DIRECTOR ACTOR COACH

*Solutions for
Director/Actor Challenges*

FORREST SEARS

DIRECTOR
ACTOR
COACH

*Solutions for
Director/Actor Challenges*

DEDICATION

In fond memory of Constance Welch

Masterful Actor Coach, Yale School of Drama

SPECIAL THANKS TO

Benedetta Toni Salerno, for her editorial assistance and continual support

&

Kevin Neighbors for his skillful editorial advisement

ACKNOWLEDGMENTS

To the gifted American and continental directors, I have studied with and been inspired by:

Joseph Anthony, Lee Bruer, Joseph Chaikin, Liviu Ciulei, Jack Clay, Morton DaCosta, Zelda Fichandler, James Lapine, John Lehne, Marshall Mason, B. Iden Payne, Oleg Tabakov and Jerry Zaks

Suggest to your actors, that in choosing their traits, they should work for subtle character changes as they move *beat* to *beat*. They should as well, find some different aspects of behavior on each new entrance. This process is sometimes referred to as, "peeling the onion", that is continuing to reveal a different layer of their character's skin. Here is a list of some major personality traits that can be helpful for your actors. Feel free to expand or abridge them to fit their needs.

Author's Note

As a graduate student at Yale School of Drama, majoring in directing, I became interested in working with actors to help solve their individual acting challenges. I had become intrigued with the expertise of Constance Welch in her acting classes as she coached us directors and acting students with ingenious exercises that solved our acting blocks.

When I began directing in my own company, I was making use of those coaching solutions in rehearsals. Later, when I worked at the Pittsburgh Playhouse as an acting teacher, I was beginning to put together exercises of my own that were helping solve my student's problems.

At the University of Idaho, I urged my student directors to search for solutions to their actor's blocks through observation, research and their own imaginations. I would assign each student specific common acting problems they had observed working with their actors. The intent was for them to create an exercise, improv, or game to attempt at solving the actor's dilemma. The most promising were tested in-class scenes. The results proved intriguing, frequently resulting in breakthroughs in the student actor's performances.

I offer you here a career-long compilation of more than 60 exercises of mine and my students, along with those of the prominent professional directors with whom I have studied in directing seminars and colloquiums. These exercises are based on the most common problems actors encounter. You will note, I have credited a few, although most are anonymous. The business of attribution is a tricky one. Most of the creators of these exercises, games, and improvs are lost in the fog of the long history of acting. Nonetheless, I have chosen to credit a few of my talented collegiate directing practitioners and prominent New York and Continental Theatre Directors.

Frankly, however, I remain reluctant to claim authorship for my own and other's exercises here. I have the whimsical notion, were I to attempt to credit every exercise, some bright theatre researcher might suddenly appear and announce, "I have a source of evidence that proves the actor Thespis used that exercise working with his actors in Ancient Greece."

These exercises are for you to discover the process of the coaching director throughout your entire rehearsal process. They exist here to be experimented with, find new aspects of and ultimately lead you to make discoveries of your own.

Forrest Sears

CONTENTS

1

The Director As Actor Coach

A coaching director is a director that goes beyond the conventional expectations of their actors. They are directors who live on the front lines with them, helping them tell a story in the most honest way possible by creating an environment where actors and directors work together to create a collaborative process, without the detachment of a sitting director, barking blocking commands and vague metaphors about feeling, story, and action. They make themselves a part of the ensemble and encourage the most extraordinary and often surprising results from their actors.

Do most directors consider themselves now or aspire to be coaching directors? I believe they do because they possess qualities of leadership, a love of acting and are highly motivated to work with actors. Should every director aim to become a coaching director? Absolutely. Coaching directors are essential in that they bridge the void of miscommunication often present between actors and directors that limit the quality and honesty of a production.

Yet, not so fast, some critical voices need to be heard. After actors have had some training and or experience is there any necessity for a director to coach them? Those who are skeptical might answer, "The director's rehearsal energies and expertise should be completely focused on other crucial directing issues of leadership, interpretation, and staging. The director needs particular gifts and skills in each of these areas. Is it realistic that they should be able to handle all this and deal with coaching the actors as well?

I would answer, "it is!" I agree the above requirements are essential, however, by using a new time-saving paradigm, offered here you achieve these required goals and are able as a coaching director to assist actors in building richer, more in-depth acting performances. "Yes", says the skeptic, "but you haven't answered my question whether an actor with experience needs all this help you are offering?"

I would reply, "Ask the actors if they believe that to be true. Were you to consult them, you would likely hear a plea from the heart for help." They might answer, "you are my audience of one, my third eye in rehearsals, and I need your coaching skills to fully discover my performance." Actors, being for the most part forgiving spirits, will likely accept their directors' benign neglect in coaching by rationalizing that they understand how overburdened they are with other responsibilities. Yet, despite that acceptance they have the need, sometimes a near desperate one, for help in solving their acting challenges.

I must speak personally and say in a five-decade directing career, I have yet to meet an actor who didn't desire, appreciate, and benefit from my or any other director's actor coaching.

Imagine a theatre audience and how a perceptive member of it might respond to a production directed by a skilled coaching director. They sense a unified acting style. Every performer, from a walk on to the leading player, would demonstrate proficiency. They recognize the actor's sense of ease in immersing themselves in their role, the result of the coaching director's emphasis on the acting craft elements of relaxation, connection, imagination, and sensory awareness. They observe their avoidance of acting clichés, allowing actors to give believable fully rounded characterizations. The actors' performances will be increasingly compelling as they reveal new layers of their characters' personalities. These are the hallmarks of the coaching director's work.

Let me share some lingering, rather entertaining, myths regarding this director. We should lay to rest one particular stereotype.

The coaching director is a controlling personality, often a frustrated actor who wants to put themselves into every role. They work not so much with the actor's emotions as they prey upon them and may manipulate them in unhealthy ways. They may be seen as a person who completely dominates another, usually with a selfish or sinister motive like the evil hypnotist Svengali in the novel, Trilby. They aim to put all their actors under their spell.

Their tactic may include haranguing an actress with threats and intimidation to induce hysteria, and when it occurs, demanding that she applies that behavior immediately in rehearsal to achieve the results of her big break down emotional scene. Such practices existed in early twentieth-century theatre.

The American director Jed Harris so attempted to manipulate actors to his personal whims that no less a talent then Laurence Olivier, whom he directed, considered his practices reprehensible. Lord Olivier later gained his revenge when he announced in his autobiography that he had based his famous portrayal of Richard III in a large part on the personality of Mr. Harris.

These earlier directors strike us today as more manipulators than coaching directors. There is no place for such behavior in today's theatre culture. Yet I should cite some incidents practiced by a few of our greatest directors of the twentieth century, which we might now consider dubious strategies.

Elia Kazan, director of a Streetcar Named Desire and Death of a Salesman, certainly one of the greatest director-coaches of the twentieth century, was brilliant in helping actors discover and release genuine emotional behavior. He was, however, sometimes prone to use Machiavellian tactics to achieve his ends. He would as a coaching tactic, ferment trouble by spreading false rumors about fellow cast members that would pit two actors, whose characters were antagonistic to each other in the script, against each other. When they came on the stage or film set, they carried their hostilities into their character relationships in the scene.

Or consider another exceptional director, Vincent Minnelli, on the set of Meet Me in Saint Louis, to "help" the young child star, Margaret O' Brien, in her emotional breakdown scene, just before the cameras rolled, lied to her that her beloved dog had just died. While these incidents have their black humor, they are rather mean spirited. So, at times, even the most gifted of directors have demonstrated behavior that perpetuates negative perceptions of the coaching director.

In today's theatre, a coaching director must be a teacher, prepared to help actors with anything from a slight suggestion to skillfully assisting them with an exercise to alleviate an acting block. While we may say all directors are teachers, they differ in their goals. The older style, sometimes called the *instructional director,* used the rehearsal hall as their classroom. They "instructed" their actors by often dictating to them their complete blocking. They would "assist" by giving them line readings and were pleased to step on the set and personally demonstrate how to play a moment, frequently, in an apologetic manner, "I'm not really an actor, but you get the idea of what I want here." This kind of teaching director still exists, although they are passing from the scene.

A fascinating irony is that the founder of modern acting, Constantine Stanislavski, who continues to inspire theatre artists, and who will be referred to often in these pages, began his career as the most authoritarian of *instructional directors,* decades before he developed his acting system. In his initial production of Chekhov's, The Seagull, he tells us of his directing preparation. He said, "I put down everything in those production notes, how and wherein what way a part had to be interpreted... what kind of inflections the actor had to use, how he had to move about and act. I described the scenery, costumes, makeup, deportment, gaits, and habits of the character. Further, he described, or more precisely choreographed, every bit of stage business or physical action. Stanislavski told the actor playing the young writer, Konstantin, that he should deliver an entire speech smoking and then instructed him when to place the cigarette in his mouth, were to inhale the smoke, and on what line to exhale it. Thirty-five years later, near the end of his career, when a young actor asked him a question about how his character might behave in a given scene, he replied, "I don't know, what do you think?" It wasn't that he was losing his creative powers, on the contrary, it was that he had a long since changed his tactics. He was no longer *instructional;* he had become a *coaching* director.

It is a commonplace for coaching directors to ask their actors questions and keep asking them, particularly in the early phases of rehearsal. I am not suggesting that they asking them out of ignorance. They should begin their rehearsals with thorough preparation concerning the play's background, history, themes, and character analysis. They will have created as well, a conceptual vision that will be their personal statement about the play.

For all this preparation, the coaching director will begin rehearsals not as the mastermind, but as the inquirer. They must be open to change. Their questions to the actors are in no way attempting to use a line of inquiry that will lead them to their preconceived ideas. They are not an attorney, slyly leading a witness into some kind of trap. Instead, they enter this questioning process with an open mind. The coaching director might say to his actors, "I am asking questions that I may not have answers for at this particular moment." While this might seem like heresy to some, the coaching director knows the actor's answers aren't definitive. They are their preliminary thoughts. What is most important is that the director asks questions to activate their mind, senses, and emotions. Further, these initial questions send a message to the actors that their input is important and that their voices will be involved in interpretation. The production will be a creative ensemble endeavor. So, as with the mature Stanislavski, coaching directors are secure in their mission. They will ask for and incorporate ideas from their actors.

It is crucial coaching directors possess a strong appreciation and an in-depth understanding of the acting process. Beginning directors will in most instances come to directing with some previous experience as a theatre artist. Whatever their former background may have been, the new director brings important skills to the job. The designer will possess essential visual skills in composition. The playwright will have a sense of dramatic structure and characterization. The director who has had considerable acting experience may seem to have an advantage but they may need to sharpen their skills in visualization and play construction. All new directors will need to build their empathy and respect for the art of acting.

The coaching director as their experience increases, will become an expert in diagnosing actor lapses. They will quickly spot moments when an actor is not listening to their partner, their imagination is not engaged, or they are working too hard or need to simplify. This director learns to identify and deal with a near-limitless number of acting challenges. They need to have a suggestion or exercise for almost any acting block they encounter. In fact, they must have multiple solutions because actors are individuals. One exercise does not fit all. An abundance of exercises, theatre games and improvisations are required to help solve actor challenges.

I will suggest here more potential solutions than you can use in a single production. This is intentional. You will choose the exercise that most appeals to you. However, know that you have more than one shot at solving the problem. If the first one misses the target, you have more ammunition to give your actor.

I need to be clear that while coaching is a major responsibility of the director, it is by no means their sole function. Practitioners of directing are in general agreement that there are four major areas of expertise essential for directing success. The first three have been extremely well-documented. A detailed discussion of them dominates the content of the many available books on directing. They cover the areas of leadership, organization, staging and text interpretation. The fourth major area-the director as actor coach-while certainly of equal importance, is less familiar territory. The outline that follows provides an overview of the requisites for a director, with our concept of an actor coach being a crucial component.

I. The Director as Organizer and Leader of the Production:

    1. The director as the unifier of all the production elements.

    2. The director as a mediator and diplomat.

    3. The director as a planner-coordinator.

    4. The director as a critic-evaluator.

    5. The director as a builder of cast morale.

II. The Director as Stager (blocking the production)

    1. The director as a storyteller

    2. The director as pictorial artist, proficient in stage composition and visual moment-by-moment storyboarding of the play's action.

    3. The director as an architect of stage space and co-creator of the ground plan.

    4. The director as a co-creator of the actor's physical behavior and stage business.

    5. The director as a coordinator of stage movement.

III. The Director as Interpreter:

    1. The director as textual interpreter, adept in script analysis.

    2. The director as evaluator of dramatic structure, knowledgeable in play construction.

    3. The director as conceptualizer, creating a personal vision of the play.

    4. The director as a student of contemporary political, social, and cultural issues, which they may incorporate in their interpretation of both new and classic plays.

5. The director as conductor, establishing the play's changing tempo and rhythms throughout the play.

6. These areas of the director's art and craft are accepted practices. The fourth major area, the director as an actor coach, while of equal importance, is less familiar.

While many experienced directors have gained insight into these coaching principles, in all likelihood, it was lacking in their initial training. Except for a few journal articles and some brief sections in directing texts, this essential area of work has been greatly neglected.

It is my hope that this book will bring these principles and coaching solutions to a broader audience and encourage further research. Let me complete this outline overview of the four essentials of directing with the major requirements of the successful coaching director.

The Director as Actor Coach

1. The director has a deep understanding of the acting process and its application.

2. The director possesses the skill to work with actors on textual circumstances to bring clarity to the play's story.

3. The director is adept at a Socratic method of asking questions of their actors to help them solve textual and craft problems.

4. The director is proficient in communicating with actors and they speak to the actor's imagination in language, sometimes imagistic and metaphor at others in precise acting process directions.

5. The director is alert to the actor's individual temperaments, understanding when they are under stress and encouragement is necessary, as well as challenging them when they are complacent to become more productive.

6. The director is trained to appreciate a character's psychology. They are skilled in guiding the actors to create honest behavior in both the spoken and subtextual aspects of a script.

7. The director understands the value of improvisations and how to use them in rehearsals to enable actors to make new character discoveries.

8. The director has an ear for the playwright's dialogue. They hear the author's music and guide their actors to find the proper tone of the play.

9. The director is adept at creating a rehearsal process that creates both positive morale and schedules the actor's time wisely.

10. The director will be a co-collaborator with their actors in blocking the play. The joint teamwork will result in more organic character actions and stronger motivated movement.

These are some of the major contributions that coaching directors bring to the production. In order to draw a clearer contrast of the differences between the traditional director and the coaching director, we need to look at the typical rehearsal process which is customarily divided into four periods consisting of reading, blocking, polishing, and run-throughs. The number of rehearsals in any one section of the work will be determined by the total number of rehearsals allotted to produce the play. Both begin rehearsals with a complete reading of the play, although their strategies will differ greatly. Coaching directors choose to have more extended exploratory rehearsals, a process I will introduce in the chapters ahead.

The traditional director, after several readings, normally begins to block the play. These directors often choose between two options. The first is to block the entire play quickly in approximately five or six rehearsals. This strategy, it advocates argue, is to sketch in all the movement to get an impression of an overall look at the outset, with the intention of fine-tuning it later. After the rapid staging is completed, a "stumble through" may be called, a complete run-through with the book in hand.

In the second option, the director may choose to move much more deliberately through the blocking period to allow the actors ample time to justify their actions and for them to evaluate their work and make necessary adjustments.

As a coaching director, I would suggest the rapid rehearsal blocking of Mr. or Ms. Speedy tends to be unproductive. As rapid blocking progresses, this director is busy correcting visual problems. Their actors are likely experiencing some memory lapses regarding their stage positions while our director is discovering new options and changing their blocking. This director finds staging a period of high creativity. They may be visually gifted and enjoy continuing to experiment with many different compositions, ever in search of the alpha stage picture. They justify this procedure, feeling that their intense experimentation is at the heart of creativity. The actors, on the other hand, may feel some adrenaline as well, but it could be the excitement akin to a rickety roller coaster ride. If *Director Speedy* prolongs the *blocking* period with seemingly endless changes, their cast may find themselves in a state of utter confusion, as in the scenario of, "What version are we running today?"

Our other director, let's call him them Mr. or Ms. *Reliable,* are far more methodical practitioners. They initially blocked the play more slowly, less erratic, or experimentally than Speedy. *Director Reliable's* original actions and movements have most likely been retained by the cast. They may now make a few adjustments, but their emphasis is on continuing to run the material. This director has a workmanlike method and there may be a calming sense about their personality. On the other hand, this "block it" and then have multiple run-throughs to "set it" strategy, may create a predictability that in its repetition, if few or no new choices are discovered, can lead to apathy in a cast, and an incomplete exploration of the text.

Director Speedy's experiments will most likely not bore their actors, although it may distress them. This director's strong visual sense is a virtue as they work on compositions that are aesthetically pleasing and effectively dramatize the action of the play. They may in time become successful coaching directors. However, they must guard against being so passionate about pictorial perfection that they do not treat their actors like cardboard cutouts.

They must not forget how much actors need their help to achieve a three-dimensional performance within the two-dimensional picture the director has created.

The next rehearsal period in the traditional directing schedule and for the coaching director as well, is often referred to as the Polishing Period. Here, the director and their actors are engaged in moment-to-moment work on the script. The quality of the rehearsals

In this middle period will be a major factor in the success or lack of it in the production. Four chapters in this book will deal with this process in-depth as it is at the heart of the coaching director's work.

The final phase, run-throughs, technical, and dress rehearsals are the last challenges in the rehearsal process. The traditional and the coaching director, will handle this period, like the others, quite differently.

As you read this model of the traditional director's goals, you may be thinking the rehearsal procedures described here may result in less than outstanding productions. Is there a better directional approach? I undertook the writing of this book to suggest there is.

Let me then preview the progression of *Actor Director Coach*. Chapters 2,3 and 4 describe the bonding exploratory period of rehearsals. The coaching director here has three major goals. The first is to establish a commonality of acting craft terms that actors and a director will share.

Chapter 2 defines and describes in-depth the ten essential acting elements that need to be active in each textual scene. These techniques establish a mutual working process to ensure precise actor/director communication. If one or more of them is missing, the director has work yet to accomplish.

The second element is the improvisation. Chapter 3 is exclusively devoted to actors experimenting with improvs in rehearsals. It is not intended as an actor training technique here but rather as a method for them, at the earliest rehearsals, to begin to work together to develop character relationships and make discoveries related to both the present and past life histories of their characters. Ten situations from well-known plays are offered to illustrate this process. You will create from your play's events, short scenarios, to explore in improvisations.

Chapter 4 *exploratory rehearsals*, is an alternative to repetitive play readings. It deals with more than 60 exercises and improvs and theatre games throughout this book. It begins by easing actors into a creative state of relaxation and then awakens their imaginations with sensory awareness work. It introduces a number of exercises for the entire cast to explore physically and emotionally together. This will strengthen the primary goal of the coaching director, creating a connected acting ensemble.

In Chapter 5, as blocking begins, we employ a new paradigm used by select professional directors, but which for the most part remains unknown. It completely breaks with traditional practice, is more efficient and challenges actors to discover important character choices earlier. The script is divided into smaller units and analyzed initially in greater depth. A five-step process is employed in which character analysis and staging occur together.

Chapter 6 deals with actors engaging their imagination by creating a series of continuous images. The book offers a series of simple exercises that, within a few minutes of rehearsal time, will spark the actor's imaginations. This process which explores the areas of personal, fantasy, and textual images will create the movie in the actor's mind that will vividly bring alive their characters.

Chapter 7 PLAYING TOGETHER offers a varied group of exercises, improvs, and games to solve the most common actor challenges, including weak concentration, lack of actor contact, connection and finally vulnerability, the need to be emotionally open and available for their partners. These are addressed in a series of original exercises.

Chapters 8 and 9 focus on psycho-physical solutions to actor challenges. This deals with Stanislavski's late discovery that suggested physical and psychological actions are symbiotic, they cannot be separated. The actor's physical movements influence their internal behaviors and motivations.

These two chapters present the first solo then ensemble exercises that will empower your actors to make stronger, more truthful textual choices.

Our keystone exercise, LIFELINE is a tactile exercise involving your entire cast. I discovered it when a major problem occurred in a final dress rehearsal. I devote Chapter 9 entirely to a description of this event and how a spontaneous solution to the problem evolved. You will find this exercise a tangible lifeline for your actors from the first off-book section of your scrips through dress rehearsals.

Chapter 10, Putting It Together, makes a plea for a well-planned, time-efficient rehearsal schedule. Specific tips on note presentations to the actors are offered. Different specific goals for the actors to achieve in each final run through are presented to help guard against complacency from frequent repetitions. The best ratio of introducing new text balanced with previously rehearsed work is explored.

These techniques, among others, will result in a rehearsal process that continues to build actor commitment and results in positive morale. I believe quality endeavors in directing is the mastery of organization, leadership, staging, concept/interpretation, and actor coaching. These four elements come together to create the superior director. The first three have been widely discussed in print, while actor coaching has not. Despite the absence of a discussion on these principles in publication, there are many practicing and gifted coaching directors working in our theatres. These actor-coaches have learned their skills through trial and error and/or mentoring with talented directors who have shared their coaching techniques. Thus, the training of actor coaches has been an essential oral tradition, until now.

2

The Ten Essentials
Of Every Scene

The Director's Score

In any scene or play, actors and directors need to consider ten essential acting principles that will provide the most valuable tools for an actor and will help them solve problems in rehearsals. Well-trained actors have dealt with them in their work, but may have become neglectful of them over time. Some of your less experienced cast members may be familiar with a few but not all of them and some beginners may come to you with a blank slate. It is important, therefore, that you are well prepared to re-kindle, augment, or teach these preparation techniques to your actors. The cumulative application of these essentials is often referred to as the plays "score". A director may be compared to an orchestra conductor. Both work from a score. One deals with musical notes, the other with spoken words. Both strive to ensure that their players give full value, color, and accuracy to their work. Missing intended musical notations or missing essential dramatic moments will impede a performance. In the annals of theater history documentation, there is a sketch of the director of a medieval morality play holding a manuscript in one hand, which he is gazing at, and a baton in the other, presumably conducting his actors in a scene rehearsal. While such a practice has been abandoned for centuries, it is still a powerful metaphor for the director working with a score.

To create a process for this procedure, I offer you a contemporary *score* with ten key elements. I strongly believe these elements need to be incorporated in every acting scene. The sequence will be geared to the flow of your rehearsal process. We will divide them into three sections. The first is: **work on the script** which includes three essentials, *Given Circumstances, backstory* and *subtext.* This is followed by **work on the self**, which is a combination of the actor's homework and rehearsal explorations as they work to solve their personal challenges. The three elements here are: *physical condition, inner objects* or *images, relationship to the other characters* and *inanimate objects.* The final group deals with **work on the character**. These components include: *psychological actions, physical actions, obstacles,* and *beats.*

These ten essentials provide your actors the necessary technique to make their characters unique. The director must likewise work on such a *score.* You will need to prepare as complete and in-depth a textual analysis as pre-rehearsal time permits. The director will also engage in this process using these ten elements in rehearsals. The sum of the actor's and director's choices creates the interpretation of the play. These ten essentials will give you the creative power to "*score*" your production.

This first three principles deal with script analysis. You will continue to work on them throughout your rehearsals. They are stepping stones in understanding a text and time is needed for them to mature properly.

I. Given Circumstances

Chances are you have dealt with this concept previously. It is impossible to have a detailed discussion of a play script and omit it. Searching for the play's circumstances is the most objective task you and your actors will undertake. It requires careful investigation. Think of it as detective work. You might equate *Given Circumstances* to the T.V. police show of an earlier era, *Dragnet*, in which the officer requested of those he questioned, "Just the facts, ma'am." Your actors should record all the facts about their characters they can discover in their scripts. Then, they need to make a list of them based on who, what, where, when, and why. Some of these facts are immediately obvious and simple. Others, at the outset, are more elusive. They can be like elements in a jigsaw puzzle; a piece in a later scene in the text can bring clarity to what was earlier unclear. You and your actors need to be vigilant in your pursuit of these "givens". If your actor ignores or misinterprets a circumstance, to shape it more to their liking or personal comfort zone, that actor isn't telling the story the playwright wrote. It is your job to make sure all your actors are playing by the same rules. As a coaching director, keep asking *what* is the meaning of a particular action, *why* is the character doing this? Keep your actors probing their characters psychological make-up.

Actors should likewise explore their *given circumstances* playwright's stage directions. There are books on acting that council the actor to cross out all of them. This I think is excessive and may rob the actor of some important objective clues that may not be available elsewhere. I do understand why an acting coach might make such a suggestion. There was a tendency for some playwrights, in the past, to instruct the actor on how to play a scene, often an emotional one. Their directions would cite the specific feelings they envisioned for a particular moment. For example, a direction might read, "slowly he crosses to the chair, turns to her with a look of vengeful fury and violently slams his fist into the cushion." This, of course, is most un-helpful; if followed it leads to playing the emotional result of the scene rather than searching for the reason for a character's *physical* and *psychological* actions. If your actors are unaware of this, counsel them to disregard the "slowly, vengeful, violently," adverbs that instruct the actor *how* to do something, when the actor should be searching instead for *what* and the *why*. What does the character need and why do they need it?

Once your actors have been counseled to disregard this kind of emotionally overwrought advice, both you and your cast may gain valuable insights into the play's characters and themes by carefully reading their playwright's stage directions.

To be certain your actors are identifying all the pertinent information from the character's past, you may want to ask them to identify and record each truthful event about their character and incorporate them in their early memorization process. In these first rehearsals, take time to be certain that each actor has identified and understands all the information concerning who they are, when it is, where it is, and why they behave as they do. The *who* and the *why* should be continuously explored and expanded by your actors throughout the entire rehearsal period.

II. Back Story

You will need to give your actors time, at least, the first week of rehearsal, to consider and organize the playwright's *given circumstances*, before they begin to expand them into the more subjective back story. This work is the actor's extension of their fact-gathering, but in this phase, it turns creative as the actor enters their imagination and begins the rehearsal's long process of making their personal character choices. The more objective circumstances the actors create, the more opportunities for imaginative backstory.

Stella Adler, the legendary acting teacher, told her students, "Your talent lies in your choices." She was suggesting the stronger, the more imaginative, and the more original choice, distinguishes the actor of talent from the less inspired player who is content interpreting the *given circumstances* without entering into this alchemy of creative acting. Indeed, if only playing the playwright's *given circumstances* were the final goal of acting, every performer would deliver essentially the same performance. How long would the theatre endure under those conditions? Audiences go to see plays with actors who make choices that live not only within, but extend the *given circumstances* of the story in bold and exciting ways.

Occasionally an actor confuses his backstory with the playwright's *given circumstances*. Do not allow your actors to play their characters to justify their creations. Backstory is not the play's narrative. It exists to heighten and clarify the background of the character based on the playwright's intentions.

While this sounds obvious, many actors, eager to engage their creativity, jump into rehearsals and start making choices based on past events in the play's plot that are their creation, inaccurate, and clash with the playwright's specific circumstances. This can only lead to problems that if present, must be corrected later. Actors must realize the wrong backstory presents a play the author didn't write.

The backstory is the character's earlier and present life events that we do not learn in the course of the play's dialogue, but consists of choices that the actor makes that empowers their performance. Skill in bringing a backstory alive is based in large part on the actor's imagination and the creation of images. There are, however, essential background questions you may offer your actors for their preparation of both *given circumstances* and *backstory*.

Who Am I?

I Physical Profile

Age (height and weight, different from the actor)

Type of speech (degree of, regional or national dialect)

Characteristic way of walking?

Level of vitality (low to high energy)?

Body center (lead from head, heart, stomach, groin)?

II Life History

Vivid early childhood experiences

Relationships to mother, father, siblings, etc. (changes in relationship?)

Educational background

Occupation

Economic level

Social life

Homelife, hobbies

Style of dress

III Behavioral

Introvert/Extrovert (rate on a scale 1-10)?

How does the character behave under emotional stress?

What is their basic outlook on life?

Behavioral problems or psychological disorders?

The Other Elementary W's

What

What did I just do before entering the scene?

What surrounds me? (Imagine the place and the inanimate objects)

What objects do I handle? What is my relationship to them?

Where

Where is the action taking place? Country, city, neighborhood, house, room, or outdoors?

When

The action is occurring in what century, year, season, month, and time of day?

Why

Do you see patterns in your past connecting to the present? Do you understand why you are behaving as you are, as the play begins?

These are some of the basic questions your actors need to be asking themselves to cultivate depth into their backstory. Some directors like to hand out a character profile list for their casts to write out. This may be helpful. I would urge however, not to allow this to be only a left-brain analytical exercise. Your actors must shift this information to their right brain, the creative side, where it ceases just being data. They must dream, envision, and physicalize these facts into their own original acting choices.

III. Subtext

There are sections in every play where the characters express their thoughts directly and honestly. Then there are playwrights whose characters rarely express verbally what they are thinking and feeling. In any given moment, their spoken words may be in 180-degree opposition to the thoughts, they are experiencing and the needs they want fulfilled. When this is happening, actors and directors must deal with the *subtext* in the scene- what is underneath the surface dialogue.

We could say a character is speaking in code and their partner(s) in the scene must de-code the message. This may be simple or it may be complex. The density or near opaqueness in a text is frequently driven by the amount of subtext in the dialogue. What is being hidden from other characters in a scene filled with hidden motives? To mistake the surface text as truth at the expense of the subtext, is misinterpreting the play. The character's reason for subtext may be appropriate, for example, to protect the listeners from information that might be harmful to them. Or it may be self-serving or even vicious.

It is interesting to note that as you and your actors search for hidden truth below a character's casual conversation, you may be thinking of a verb that discloses their actual intention. Verbs, of course, imply action. Later in this section on actor essentials, we will discuss *PSYCHOLOGICAL ACTIONS*. This principle is at the center of Stanislavski's acting system. It is the best way for the actor to discover the hidden intentions or subtext in a scene.

Take an example of an important sub-text from Anton Chekhov, a playwright noted for his keen skill and application of it. In his play *The Seagull*, we encounter a character whose intention is to conceal a habit. Masha is a young woman with a substance abuse problem. In a scene in which she is likely intoxicated from vodka, she rises, from talking with a friend seated on a lawn, stumbles, and says, "My foot has gone to sleep." Obviously, she is not concerned about exercising her foot back to normal, but rather in attempting to stand up straight and conceal her inebriation. It is the subtextual intention of, I must hide my drinking problem. This concealed intention is most important at this moment and is what the actress must work to accomplish. "My foot has gone to sleep", is merely a subterfuge rather than the crucial information.

As we conclude this first section of the ten essentials, devoted to script analysis, based on *given circumstances, backstory* and *sub-text* be aware this is an ongoing process you will explore with your actors throughout the rehearsal period.

Backstory should be enriching your actors each time they work on a scene. It is their private work on their character's life. As such it may prove one of the richest sources the actor has to create a characterization somewhat or enormously different from other actors who have played the role. Backstory is an actor's unique invention; they should use it to ignite their creative imagination. Urge your actors throughout rehearsals to keep filling in new pages of their character's life story.

Subtext is perhaps the most challenging aspect of script analysis. As a director, you need to be alert to any of your actors who aren't digging for clues beneath the surface of the text. Help them find the buried treasure of their character; convince them of the wealth of new choices subtext can provide them.

Some of your less experienced actors may assume sub-text is appropriate in serious drama and some classics, but isn't present in modern comedies or farces. Actually, it is in the modern plays of all genres. From the late 19th century onward, playwrights, in sync with the development of psychology, have given a special emphasis to their character's needs, drives, strengths, and disorders and their inclinations to hide them. In short, motivation, the why of human behavior, has taken on increased importance. Directors must encourage their actors to become psychological sleuths. I would caution you not to expect your casts to decode the full subtext in their earliest encounters with a scene. You are the final authority on the interpretation of each beat or moment of the text. If you judge in a rehearsal, your actor's choices to be appropriate, at this moment in rehearsal, you will choose to move on.

There is always plenty of work ahead. However, I would suggest you avoid determining early solutions as conclusive in interpreting subtexts. Plays can be ambiguous and have the potential for multiple meanings. Ask your actors to experiment, try different ideas, and investigate deeply. If the initial choice made proves to be the best one, they will, of course, return to it. On the other hand, you haven't wasted time by experimenting with other options and allowing your actors the possibility of finding one more exciting and appropriate than the first. This is a better strategy than in late rehearsals discovering that a choice made a month ago now seems wrong and they have to re-think and re-work a scene when time is running short

Work on the Self

In this section of the essentials, we will be looking at the actor's inner process. The following four essentials are about the preparation they will need to do between rehearsals and what they bring to the next one. You will work with actors at different levels of experience and types of training. You must understand the actor's process to assist them, when acting challenges arise.

IV. Physical Condition

You should suggest to your cast the importance of concentrating on a simple physical reality in their time on stage. Most often, it should be the first step in their preparation before making an entrance. *Physical condition* may be thought of as the character taking their emotional temperature in the most basic way. "I am warm", "I feel cold." Most of the time it is the character physicalizing the *given circumstances* of the scene. There are exceptions to this, in a highly charged emotional moment, the character might experience a *physical condition*, that is a sense experience contrary to the given of the text. Say a character who is outside in zero-degree weather suddenly threatened at gunpoint, their *physical condition* may change from cold to hot, sweating from an adrenaline rush. Your directorial obligation with *Physical Condition* is to be certain that your actors have an appropriate sensory choice that mirrors the emotional requirements of the scene. If it is missing, you need to suggest a simple sense experience with which they can connect. The need for such a technique is twofold. First, when your actor taps into a sensory reality that is analogous to the mood of the scene, they strengthen their belief in that moment. As acting coaches are fond of saying, "it allows the actor to drop into the here and now."

The second virtue of this process is spectator related. Atmospheric elements such as heat, cold, dry throat, windburn, sunburn, sweaty palms, itchy scalp, fever, and chills are so universally experienced by every human being, they are highly recognizable to the point of audience empathy. The spectators not only relate to the *physical conditions* but may begin to experience them in their bodies. This, then serves as a strong "hook" to pull the audience into the world of the play. Because this is such a seemingly basic technique, both actors and directors often overlook it.

V. Images and Inner Objects

I labeled the beginning of this section *Work on Self;* I am suggesting this sequence is the actor's homework away from rehearsals. This does not imply that you are not involved. The director should take a strong hand in monitoring it. How do directors monitor and what is involved with *Images and Inner Objects?* The actors find their own particular, personal moments from their fantasy or their life experience that provide stimulus in the scene that they are playing. The point is, your actors must be actively pursuing inner experiences that generate behavior appropriate to the script moment to moment.

There is a belief by some that images are always visual pictures. A famous textbook on acting titles a chapter on them, "Seeing Things". I think a far more accurate description would be "Experiencing Things". Images may be pictures but they can be other sensory elements as well, taste, touch, smell, or sound. The essential thing, and this is where you will monitor the process, the actors must be engaged in an ongoing attempt of experiencing stimuli that create a truthful performance.

You are your actor's guide to help them make this happen; you will need to observe any signals of difficulty. Look in your actor's eyes. Are they neutral and empty or are they alert and sending messages to their partners? Does he have the breath to empower what he is saying? What is the body language? Slack with nervous unnecessary mannerisms? Or still and energized with spine involvement? If you are seeing any negative factors, don't hesitate to use the phrase with which Stanislavski frequently admonished his actors, "I don't believe you."

When you observe an actor in a static state, stalled and uninvolved in the demands of the scene, you need to stop the action and assist them. They have become disconnected from the text. You must get their motor running again.

This is when your work with imagery should come into play. It is generally not wise to give actors an image you have personally experienced. It ideally should arise from their private imaginative world. You can be helpful by offering analogies. You might say to an actor in a scene, where intense frustration is dominant, "it is as if there is an emergency for you to drive an injured friend to the hospital. You turn the ignition key and realize your battery is dead." Be available for your actor with vivid suggestions if the light behind their eyes turns off or worse, if it is yet to turn on at all.

This, then is an introductory description of the actor's imagery and why it is essential in every scene. I will explore the process in detail in chapter 6.

VI. Relationships with the Other Characters

You need to be alert to character relationships and the shifting nature of them throughout a play. They are a powerful source of psychological richness and storytelling values. The coaching director knows that character relationships are not generic. The play does not deal with the mother, the brother, the son, or the uncle. It deals with three-dimensional characters in relationships that are always in flux. As you work with your actors making decisions about their relationships, beware of "No". Negativity is no more attractive on the stage than it is in life. As you discuss character motives with your actors, be extremely skeptical of them making any negative choices.

Why do so many acting teachers and directors repeat to their actors what has become a theatre mantra, "play to win"? Because to play to lose, to give up, to say no, can shut down the plot; it can end the play's rising action. When there is no further opportunity for the characters to exercise new strategies to gain what they want to achieve, the actor has forfeited the possibility for further growth and change, which is intrinsic in all playwriting. In any genre, from tragedy to farce, the actors should not allow their characters to give up their struggle to succeed.

The actor playing Willy Loman in *Death of a Salesman* must not make the negative choice; "I am a loser and want to kill myself." Rather he chooses suicide because, "I want my son, Biff to inherit my insurance and have an opportunity for a successful life." This may, indeed, be morally the wrong choice but from Willy's point of view it is not a negative, but an enabling one. There is potential power in yes! "Yes" by no means signals concession or defeat. Rather, it suggests timeout as the character ponders new strategies to win their needs in the next beat.

Your actors should know all the possible information available about the other characters. They should have a vivid back story about each of them. Have them start with a positive attitude toward them if the text permits it. Directors often tell actors to find the love in a scene. This may open the opportunity for changing and conflicting relationships to follow. In well-written plays, as in life, relationships do not remain static, they are in a state of continual change. Finding the love for another character does not imply that it's permanent. A scenario might be: surface text, "I love you", subtext, "but I must lie to you to achieve my needs." This leads to ever-changing relationships-disappointment, hostility, forgiveness, and restored love, then the cycle begins all over again.

In character relationships, the more contradictions, or 180- degree turns in behavior, actors can find in a scene, the richer it will be. Council your actors to be open to the possibility that relationships may change in the next beat of the play. Help them to banish "no" and embrace, "yes", find friendship and love, know that can change, and discover its progression.

VII. Relationship with Inanimate objects

As a director you have such a wealth of organic details to deal with at every rehearsal, it is easy to overlook the inorganic ones. I am referring to key objects or props with which characters have a relationship that requires the actor's emotional and/ or psychological commitment created in their *back-story*. In Ibsen's *Hedda Gabler,* the stage directions read: "over the sofa, on the wall of the back inner room hangs a portrait of Hedda's father, General Gabler." The picture seems to dominate the room and continues to dominate Hedda. The actress playing the role must have an in-depth back story about the painting. When was it created? Was it a gift to Hedda from her father? She observes it frequently during the play's action. Ibsen wants us to understand how much the deceased military man's control continues to influence the strong but neurotic behavior of his daughter. Hedda's relationship to the General's visible picture on stage throughout the play, is equally as important as that she has with any of the live characters in the drama. The actress must create as complete a back story, as possible suggesting his crucial influence on her life.

In Tennessee Williams, The Glass Menagerie, the severely introverted and isolated Laura Wingfield, has a powerful relationship with several objects in the living room of her mother, Amanda, where there is an old wind up Victrola and a stack of aging wax records. Laura plays this music frequently. Why? Your actress Laura will need a detailed *backstory* so she can endow these inanimate objects with the appropriate emotional reality to make them as vivid as the live characters in the play. Whose Victrola is it? Was it her fathers? Did he give it to her? What associations does each of the songs have for her? Do they evoke for Laura happier memories of the past before her father left the family? Are they memories of school days, perhaps fanta-sized romantic attachments like the one she has with Jim O'Connor, her soon to be gentleman caller? Whatever choices your actress makes, it will enrich those moments when she plays the Victrola and invests her imaginative life into a relationship with the music.

The second object of Laura's near-total absorption is the glass menagerie, her collection of miniature glass blown animals. This is the private world that she has constructed. Unlike the Victrola music, which most likely has some connections to her real life, the glass animals are created entirely from her fantasies. Does she enter into the animal's world? Does the unicorn interact with the other animals or is he a loner like Laura? Those might be the initial questions your Laura should ask and then answer for herself, in her acting journal.

We come now to that *essential,* which in all likelihood will dominate your work as a coaching director from early to final rehearsals. It would be impossible to have a serious exchange concerning character interpretation without a discussion of this element. It is your actors need to search out their characters, actions, intentions, needs, goals, verbs, purpose or objectives. These are all, unfortunately, synonyms to describe this process. This *psycho-logical action,* existing in every acting scene, leads the actor to discover both the core meaning of the scene as well as leading to the through-line of the play, it's overall theme.

This is the compass that keeps the actors work on course. Throughout the entire rehearsal process, the coaching director should be assisting their actors to define, refine, strengthen, and then simplify their characters *psycho-logical actions.* These actions are always in the form of a verb. It is the search of discovering the precise verb to map out what the actor's character wants, needs, or must-have from the other character(s) in a scene.

These verbs, which the actors are searching for, will likely be in a contin-ual state of flux throughout the rehearsal process. The actors must seek to develop their characterizations with the strongest, most specific verbs their imagination and intellect can produce.

Searching for psychological action is one of the foundations of Stanislavski's acting system. It is arguably the most well-known and near-universally accepted of all his principles. I question, however, if it is practiced by directors to the degree that it might, given its proven results in giving actors this powerful tool to interpret their roles. You may have been previously introduced to this concept. If you have not, I urge you to discover its value and apply it in your directing. If you are familiar with Stanislavski, "Units and objectives," and find it intriguing, but for whatever reason have not yet applied it to your directing craft, I beg, beseech, entreat, implore, you to do so. Yes, there is power in strong action verbs.

For your actors who have not worked with *psychological actions,* council them to express their verb in the first-person singular using the words I want, I need or I must according to the degree of the urgency of their action. A teenager asking his father to borrow the family car might be making a polite request when he says, "I *want* to drive the car tonight" while, his "I *must* drive the car tonight" suggests a more intense or perhaps an emergency. The actor must have a "because" in mind for the action he is taking. "*I must* drive the car tonight because it will impress my date." The *psychological action* deals with the elementary "W" questions, what, and why. They are the tools that drive the dramatic story forward and reveal the characters intentions and motivations. That is why we will call them *psychological actions.* They are best revealed through action verbs. A helpful book, *The Actors Thesaurus* states it well. They use, "A transitive or active verb that you can actively do to someone else. It is always in the present tense…. expressing an action that carries over from you the subject to the person your speaking to (the object)." The *psychological action* needs to have urgency and a strong expectation that it will be successfully achieved. In the next directing essential, ahead, we shall see there are frequently problems preventing that from happening.

Consider your role as the coaching director as the great encourager. Throughout the work with your actors, you will urge them to make stronger, more powerful action verb choices. Keep asking what, who and how. What do you want, from whom do you want it? How are you going to get it?

How should this process proceed? Some directors ask their actors to "score" their entire role. They should choose every verb, as their character's intentions change throughout the play. Other directors might attempt that task themselves; writing in their script, each character's verbs moment by moment so they may provide every actor a choice, if and when needed. For either actor or director, this is a formidable endeavor.

Further, it is, I believe an exercise in futility, particularly because the verbs should be changing throughout rehearsals, growing in power as both the actor and director gain further insight into the characters. There should be both thought and preparation on action verbs away from rehearsals. The most effective strategy, however, would seem to be a collaboration of choices made in the rehearsal process as you challenge your actors with the questions that lead them to discover their character's strongest *psychological actions.* Caution your actors that not all verbs are playable. Remind them a verb must be doable. It must have the power to incite a possible change in the character's situation and it must be received and responded to, by the partner. The esteemed actor coach, Lee Strasberg, was said to have six favorite power verbs that he felt covered a large scope of human behavior and suggested them frequently. They are: to dominate, to destroy, to seduce, to accuse, to celebrate and to beg or plead. William Ball, an American Director, suggested a longer list of super verbs. They include: to hurt, inspire, suppress, incite, crush, encourage, lambast, ensnare, tease and reassure among others.

These lists are not intended to be definitive. As your actors work in this process, they will discover their potent verbs that will work well as they select their *psychological actions.* These verbs are frequently not the actor's first choice. They are the result of a rehearsal process of trial and error in which the actors progress from initial weaker verbs, incapable of prying opens a change in the character's needs, to those that can incisively alter another character's behavior in a scene. I suggest both the director and actors in rehearsals choose some preliminary *psychological actions* without, a pre-planned score of verb choices. Both directors and actors need to have confidence that creativity will often be born out of spontaneity. This process will be enormously enhanced by the coaching directors' questions.

Remember, the director does not need to know the answer to every question or the perfect verb for every moment. Your most important role is asking the right questions that trigger discovery for your actors.

There is a particular connection between our acting essential, subtext, and the *psychological action*. I have mentioned that in plays of complexity, when we first begin to work on them, we may sense a deeper meaning behind the dialogue, but at the moment it is inaccessible to us. Often the *psychological action* can solve the puzzle.

As actors and directors discard early verbs for stronger more powerful ones, they often gain sudden insight into the *subtext* and consequently the playwright's intention.

Take Masha in Chekhov's, *The Seagull*, at the moment she rises and stumbles. In early rehearsals, the actress might interpret her *psychological action* as, "I must adjust my foot that is asleep." As she gains more insight into the script, she will change her verb to I must leave" (because I am drunk)."

You will provide major help to your actors in their discovering both textual and subtextual *psychological actions* by persistently asking the same questions using the verbs *get* and *make*. Director William Ball would ask his actors: "What are you trying to *get* from him? Or, "what are you trying to *make* him give you?"

The answer must, Ball said:

1. "Contain a *verb,* I am trying to *convince.*
2. Contain a *receiver;* I am trying to *convince him.*

3. Contain a *desired response*. I am trying *to convince him* to go with me." *

Here are five reminders to share with the actors. Psychological Actions should be:

1. Active not passive
2. Winning not losing
3. Specific not general
4. Bold not weak
5. Positive, not negative

VIII. Physical Actions

I prefer referring to what Stanislavski has called the objective of the *psychological action* because this process needs to be discovered in tandem with the physical action. In the actor's process, psychological and physical actions work off each other in a complementary way in rehearsals. The psychological action-the verb- is conceived in the mind: the physical action comes from the body. The actors' mind triggers their body to spontaneous action. The earliest staging moments should explore the analytical, the psychological action verb and the physical actions, what the actor does, *working with them together in the same rehearsal.* This is a break from traditional directing strategies that tend to work on the *physical actions* of blocking almost immediately but often waits days or longer, before discovering the psychological actions of character behavior.

Physical actions may be defined as the actors' motivated movements and the behavioral physicalizations they may add. For example, you may direct an actor to cross to the armchair downright, pick up the evening paper from the table next to it, sit and begin to read it. The actor does so and then might choose to add his physical behavior which could be to take from his pocket a pair of wire glasses, carefully bend the bows to fit behind his ears, put them on, and clears his throat as he picks up the papers and turns to the sports section.

Physical action like the other essentials we have examined, clarify the play's story, and further reveal character. As the director, you will make the final call as to the kind and amount of physical activity in a scene. You will acquire the skills necessary to determine the degree of movement, a given scene requires. If you fail to respond to several significant action impulses in the playwright's words, your scene will be static.

On the other hand, an overabundance of *physical activity* may confuse and or tire an audience. If your actors move excessively about with little or no motivation from the script, particularly on lines that reveal the plot or move it forward, the audience will miss essential information, become confused, and may lose interest in the production.

Directors should be concerned about the overabundance of *physical actions* in their production. We may need to monitor the actor's physical mannerisms, often unconscious on their part that becomes repetitive and can be distracting to an audience. Their extraneous physical actions need to be removed with surgical precision. These physical idiosyncrasies may be lifetime habits, deep-seated in their personality. One of the worst things you can do in front of a cast is to give a note that calls attention to an actor's mannerisms in a derogatory manner. I have observed directors describing an actor's physical habit, aimed at getting a laugh from the company, with remarks like, "That thing you do with your tongue on your cheek looks like your clucking like a chicken." Sensitivity is crucial when an actor has distracting physical quirks. It is wiser to offer these notes privately to actors. As an effective coaching director, you should always try to offer an alternative *physical action* when depriving an actor of a disruptive habit.

Since personal mannerisms are often the result of tension, the director coach may suggest a relaxation image or an object (prop) for the actor to handle and displace the recurring mannerism.

I suggest in your directing you invest in the concept of stillness which has in selected moments, long been a secret of great performers. Less is more, when it comes to physical actions.

IX. The Obstacle

An obstacle can be defined as what is in the way of what a character wants in a scene. It works in conjunction with the psychological action.

When you ask your actors to identify the psychological action with an appropriate verb, ask as well for the obstacle. What may be preventing their character from obtaining what they need from other characters? This must be clear before further work of the material is possible. When your actors have discovered the obstacle, they can then frame their character's specific strategies and tactics to try to overcome it.

Without an obstacle, the characters would, from the outset of the play get everything they desired in their story. The play resolved, the actors would take a curtain call, the house lights would come up and the audience would go home after ten minutes. Clear obstacles thwarting a character's needs, keep the audience in their seats. What general principles can guide us to identify obstacles? Students learn early in their study of literature, that there are four types of plot conflicts:

1. Man, against man.
2. Man, against nature
3. Man, against the universe (fate vs. free will)
4. Man, against himself

All of the above areas are possible choices for the actor. If a single *obstacle* continues through a series of the play's *beats* in a scene, that obstacle needs to grow in intensity.

You can aid your actors by suggesting that in complex plays, a character may be dealing with multiple kinds of obstacles. The character *Hamlet*, for example, grapples with man against man, as he understands King Claudius, is his mortal enemy, whom he must kill. He feels as well, blocked by the Danish society, in his suspicions of all the characters who surround him. Further he suffers from his conflicting philosophical beliefs between man's fate and his free will. And finally, he is a man against himself as he hesitates and cannot bring himself to kill the king. Varying layers of obstacle choices give your actors a greater breadth. Choosing the best obstacles or a combination of them is essential in their work.

X. The Beat

The "beat" is a familiar term in modern actor training. Almost every acting text of the last half-century has discussed them. Yet, beats are frequently neglected in director training. They need to be a major directorial tool in the artistic crafting of a scene.

How should coaching directors make use of this technique? They should first be aware that *beats* always occur in conjunction with the previous three essentials, the *psychological action*, the *physical action*, and the *obstacle*. We can define a *beat* as a completed moment of an ongoing conflict in which two or more characters are engaged.

A common analogy is the *beat* is to the play, what a paragraph is to writing. In an essay an idea has been introduced and explored. In drama, it has been discussed or debated. At the end of a paragraph or *beat*, this idea has been accepted, rejected, or will continue and be explored from a new angle.

In either case there is first a brief pause. In writing it is identified by the visual indentation on the page. In acting, we call it a beat change. The actors pause and make an adjustment that is they take a breath which results in a physical action that can involve obvious movement or be so subtle it is near imperceptible. The characters then peruse a new psychological action, a different active verb to get what they want in the new beat from their acting partner(s).

The progression of beats is like a boxing match on stage. Two or more characters are jabbing away at one another. Each has different needs and expectations. Their differing goals or *psychological actions* produce obstacles that stand in their way of getting what they want. What they do as they continue to seek their needs is to strategize about the tactics they will employ.

That is, they will activate a different powerful action verb. So, they choose *to captivate, to confound, to seduce, to insult, to frustrate,* or *to mend*? The boxer/ actor plays out each *round/beat* with jabs, punches, slaps, embraces, kisses, whatever actions (psychological and physical) appropriate to their particular verb. Two results are possible. In the first there is a decisive victory, one character wins the other loses. Then both players return to their respective corners of their minds to plan their next strategy. A round has been finished; a complete *beat* has been played out.

In the second result, the round is a draw. Neither character has won nor lost but the will to win remains. As they pause to catch their breath, the fighters/actors plan what they will do differently in the next *round/beat* to achieve what they have been seeking.

Unlike a traditional boxing match of fifteen rounds, a full-length play may have hundreds of *beats* or more. The procedure, however, is the same. The actors/pugilists engage in conflict for what they need. Fight until they win or there is an impasse. Take a moment to plan a new attack and begin again.

Here is where you the director, are essential. Insist that your actors at the end of the *beat*, momentarily stop the action, pause, breathe, and get an image of what they want to do next and how they are going to do it. Only then are they ready to play the next *beat*. Untrained actors tend to play through beats. That is, they do not pause or make the transitional change of discovering both a new *psychological* and *physical* action that is required for the audience's complete comprehension. It only takes a few minutes of slipshod rushing through *beats* by actors before the audience is confused or lost in the play's storyline.

It is imperative that you communicate to your cast that every *beat* changes into a new one but requires some duration of silent time before it begins. The length of the pause will be variable, depending upon the amount of conflict the actor's character is experiencing.

Your task here is to be certain your actors are aware of where each new beat begins and where it changes. The most effective way for them to accomplish this is to put brackets around the beginning and end of each beat. Well trained actors prepare their scripts with enough white space. At the beginning of each new beat, the actor should list their *psychological* and *physical* action as well as the obstacle of the *beat.* Their verbs and actions can easily be forgotten if they are not recorded.

Encourage your casts to enjoy each juicy morsel of a text rather than experiencing acute indigestion by devouring too much of the feast at once. It was Stanislavski who first used food imagery to explain the *beat* process. He compared the play text to a holiday roast that the actor must carve carefully one slice at a time. A *beat* should be seen as a small part of the whole. Each *beat* is related to the super-objective of the play. That is the major *psychological* action the character is attempting to achieve. This continuity of *beats* can aid your actors to discover the plays through line of action to the super-objective.

One great values of the individual beat are the satisfying results it delivers. Working *beat* by *beat* rather than attacking the whole roast or even large sections of it, is a far more precise and productive way to work.

As we conclude this discussion of the Ten Essentials of Every Scene, we need to be aware of these principles in every rehearsal. They will offer clues to your actor's challenges and they will lead you to the appropriate exercises in this book that will hopefully solve these problems.

You may not work specifically with them all at the beginning. By run-throughs, however, you should mentally click off each of them as you are satisfied your actors are creatively applying them.

Consider these ten principles, the coaching director's toolbox. Don't go through the rehearsal door without them. Their value will only grow as your appreciation of them deepens. They will serve you both to interpret the text, tell the playwright's story more clearly, and aid you in solving your actor's problems. I urge you to keep these tools sharp.

3

Improvisation

Improvisation in this chapter is about actors working in a mutually vulnerable state, reaching out to one another spontaneously as they make character discoveries together. As the actors try their characters on to feel how they fit, it can be enlightening as a broader view of the overall world of the play emerges for them.

In advance of these sessions, you will have written a series of short scenarios of events that occur in the play, or verified circumstances from the character's past, as well as circumstances spoken of, that take place off-stage during the play's action. Give your actors a few minutes to prepare. Allow several groups to work on these ideas: they should run approximately three to five minutes. Let your actors prepare simultaneously, to save time.

These improvs should begin immediately after preliminary readings of the text. They may continue in later rehearsals when actors have gained greater mastery of their roles and will perhaps make more in-depth choices but I have persuasive reasons for your actors to engage in improvs as rehearsals begin.

Having your full cast participate at these sessions in the earliest days of rehearsals is a special opportunity for the company to get better acquainted and begin working together. This is an opportunity for you to demonstrate the important guidelines of the coaching director. Let them know you are not yesterday's instructional director and that their creative choices will be an important part of your directing process. During this session, every actor should be encouraged, when not participating in an improv, to comment on the textual choices that their fellow actors make in each presentation.

The actor's critiques of each other should essentially be focused on the play's *given circumstances*. Are the actors finding the most important events and are they integrating these objective facts of the play correctly? Incorrect perceptions of any of the playwright's text by some of your actors would not be uncommon at this stage in the process. Allow the cast to make corrections of one another if they can justify them in the text. You, of course, have done extensive research and know the text well and are the final arbitrator of the play's *given circumstances*. You should offer crucial information at these sessions as needed.

This initial improv exploration is an ideal opportunity for eliminating actor inhibitions. You will coax them to work together, planting the seeds for creating a true ensemble production, which should be the aim of every coaching director. You are sending the message to your actors that we all are here in a democratic forum, not the closed schoolroom of the instructional director. Again, it is essential that every actor, whether a minor supporting role or walk on is part of this experience. You should make every effort to create improvs that include all your supporting players.

The actors will profit from this experimental work as you guide it as a process of greater discovery of the text, not an acting critique. You must make clear to them that these improvs are not about in-depth acting performances but rather a deeper investigation of all the play's events and potential *backstories*. Be certain your approach is positive and non-judgmental so that your actors have the freedom to experiment. After each improv, ask the participants what they discovered. Did they make any breakthroughs about their character or the events in the scene? Were there changes in feelings about their relationships with other characters? Did they feel what they said and did was true to their character or would they alter some moments of it if they were to repeat the improv? Then ask the entire cast how what they heard and saw might influence their own character's relationships and interactions with the other actors.

A further value in creating the improvs in front of the entire cast is it should conclude with all the actors in agreement concerning the essential events of the plot so they are all ready to tell the play's story accurately. Another value in these early improvs is that your actors have not yet memorized their lines. After memorization, improvisations can be challenging as the learned text may conflict with the actor's spontaneity.

In the improv exercises that follow, I have chosen many well-known plays and characters involved in their textual challenges, then offer solutions to those problems. The titles of each of the exercises ahead either indicate or suggest the textual problem it is intended to solve.

Observe that your actors are working spontaneously in the moment. You should remind them that they must not pre-prepare dialogue or plan the ending of an improv.

Exercise #1
Where and When

In beginning the improvisation process, it is often helpful to work with the opening scene of the play. While it may not contain many characters, essential given circumstances occur here and need to be clarified. With the entire company watching this process, you can suggest to them they will need to incorporate some basic choices when they enter into an improv. I am referring to the "elementary w's" again, specifically, where and when. It is essential for the audience's clarity that actors communicate those specific circumstances as well as the atmosphere of the scene at the opening of the play.

Let us say you are directing *Death of a Salesman*. Your Willy Loman, has read the first scene several times, but has not yet begun to memorize it. Putting this scene into his own words should be a relatively simple way to ease into improvisation. Your actor might experience these feelings and actions as he enters into the improv.

Willy, a traveling salesman, has returned home unexpectedly from a road trip, as he fears his inability to concentrate on his driving.

As you begin the improv, ask Willy to initially focus his concentration on where he is, the time of day, and how these two elements affect him.

Your actor may begin by wearily lifting two suitcases containing his samples. They are heavy and Willy may seem to buckle under their weight. His mind wanders back to the past, as it has all day, to when as a young man how easy and pleasurable it was carrying those bags. It was a symbol of pride in his profession.

Now, years later, he is bone-weary and after a few steps toward his front door, he puts down the bags that are straining his muscles. He looks around and breathes a sigh of relief as he takes in the familiar sights, sounds, and smells of home.

He might rub his chafed hands together from the abrasive handles of his cases. He feels some momentary relief from the pressures and fears of his day.

As he looks about, in his mind's eye, he may see the neighborhood at an earlier time some twenty-five years ago. There were several beautiful trees then that have since been cut down. He takes in the comfort of that memory as he recalls their fragrance, but is saddened at their loss. Then he is jolted back to the present.

Although it is a gentle spring night, Willy feels a chill in his shoulders that spreads throughout his body. He looks at his watch and is disturbed to see that it is 1:30 am. He is bewildered by his loss of time today and particularly his inability to account for his long drive home, as he is unexpected by his wife.

What will he tell Linda? As he picks up his bags, they seem even heavier as he stumbles to the front door, unlocks it, and enters. This example of a solo improv for Willy Loman is a vivid example of a shifting *where and when* that blends past and present and propels the actor into the world of the play.

Willy is now equipped with the events and physical condition necessary to begin creative work. The actor could play this improv either as a silent inner monologue or by talking aloud to himself, a trait Willy demonstrates frequently throughout the play.

Starting with *where and when* allows actors who may have limited improv experience to find a safe place to begin. Encourage your actors at these sessions to be comfortable and relaxed. Assure them they do not need to vocally fill the entire theatre or rehearsal hall.

Your directorial skill is needed here to be the best listener present, so you can identify any cast members who are focused in their heads or inventing the next line before they speak. Urge them to genuinely hear what their partner is saying and spontaneously adjust to it.

Let your actors know they may at this early period mix their own words with those of the playwright's if they are somewhat familiar with the text. In such a mixture, the actors are taking the first steps in identifying with and personalizing their characters.

In conjunction with developing the play's where and when, the greatest advantage of improvising the opening scene of a play is for your actors to determine the text's préliminaire situation.

Most effective plays begin with major characters in a state of unstable equilibrium. The characters are not involved in any state of crisis, but the potential for it is imminent.

The director as a storyteller must be sure the specifics of the play's crucial information of the play's exposition is vividly clear to the audience.

As you improv the opening scene of *Death of a Salesman*, it should be made clear that Willy is fighting problems that could ultimately lead to a mental break down. You should work to help your actors identify strongly with the play's events and the moments before, they enter a scene.

Exercise #2

First Meetings

Great drama and comedy hinge on how past events in the characters' lives affect their present given circumstances. Help your actors find key events in their characters' pasts that trigger their current behavior.

Investigate this by improvising major characters' first meetings with each other, before the action of the play begins. In this work encourage them to create their backstories as rehearsals continue. As your actors explore their first encounters, they should experience the initial chemistry, feelings, and impressions of each other. How are their personalities alike or strongly contrasting?

If you are working on a play like *Death of a Salesman*, where a first meeting is not specified, you will want to explore relationships such as Willy and his wife Linda. Pay attention to the events that define their characters, for instance Linda Loman's unwavering love and loyalty for Willy.

Ask the characters to go back forty years to when they first met. Linda might be working as a receptionist for the Wagner Company, the firm that has recently hired the young salesman, Willy Loman.

She is immediately intrigued by this new employee who frequently strides confidently past her desk into the boss's office. He finds the young woman extremely attractive. He hasn't missed her persistent smiles and attempts to engage her in conversation.

The boss has given Willy two tickets to a Broadway show. He asks Linda for a date and she accepts. They enjoy the play and each other's company. To get better acquainted, Willy suggests they stroll through Central Park.

On the walk he might tell her of his pride in being a salesman and that he considers it a remarkable profession. He might share with her that his inspiration has come from an older salesman he has met on the train. Willy tells her, this man, Dave Singleton, 84-years-old, sits in his hotel room in green velvet carpet slippers, and calls his buyers and receives every order because his clients have built such affection for the old man.

He explains Singleton is his idol for this perfect career. Linda is moved by the story and his enthusiasm. A mutual attraction begins as they continue their walk.

While this incident of the first date does not occur in the play, the story of Dave Singleton does and that could offer strong motivation to the improvisation. The actors will build a bridge of circumstances, both textual and invented, that allows them to make imaginative connections from the past into present moments in the script.

In creating your improv scenarios, you will work to meld an invention of the character's backstories with the playwright's *given circumstances* to aid your actors in making imaginative choices.

Exercise #3
Crucial Character Events

Turn again to *Death of a Salesman*. The original director, Elia Kazan, called the play "a love story between a father and son." To clarify that relationship, with all its ambivalences, it would be valuable to consider improvising two scenes, peripheral to the action, that again, do not occur onstage.

The first improv springs from a reference to the Ebbets Field locker room. Willy and his family arrive to watch his son Biff play his high school football championship game. You might create a situation in which Willy has followed his son into the locker room for a private moment to share his love and pride.

Willy, full of grandiose plans and bravado, sketches out his secret play to help Biff score in the game. This situation may provide some humor, but more importantly it could help shape the camaraderie between father and son in this flashback.

With the same characters, try improvising the results of later events that build tension between them. This happens after Biff travels to Boston where Willy is on the road working. Biff has come to tell his father that he has flunked math and consequently won't be offered a college athletic scholarship. The son discovers, on barging into his father's hotel room, that Willy is involved in a sexual relationship with another woman. The image of the father he has hero-worshipped is shattered.

The two actors might now create an improvisation, not in the play that would take place at home a short time later. Willy knocks on Biff's bedroom door and asks to talk with him about his high school situation. Biff reluctantly allows his father to enter the room. Willy pleads with his son to urge his teacher to change the failed grade or that he takes the math class in summer school, so he will be eligible for an offered scholarship. Biff stubbornly refuses. Tempers may flare. Both characters may air accusations.

I would suggest here, where a guilty secret is at the heart of the conflict, that you counsel your actors not to speak specifically of it in the improv. The woman in Boston is the subtext the men are avoiding. It can become a stronger obstacle and consequently help the actors discover greater tensions in the scene, if the source of the problem is unspoken.

In creating the improvs for your next production, think of key situations at the outset, near the crisis, and the climax of the play. By doing so you give your actors the opportunity at the beginning of rehearsals to grasp high points of their characters' story and to experience the journey of their character, throughout the play.

Exercise #4
News of the Day

Directors face some challenges in interpreting period plays set in historical times other than our own. Be prepared to do considerable research on a play whose history and/or culture is unfamiliar to you.

One of the perks of directing is the lifetime education you provide yourself as you become immersed in the history, customs, manners, and politics of plays of all periods. This knowledge is of course not just about your acquisition of it. You need to find the best manner to communicate it to your actors.

You may speak to your cast about the play's historical background, as well as assign specific topics for your actors to study and share with the rest of the company. You can search out the best visual documentaries to illustrate a particular era to show your actors. You can bring in local experts to speak. Any approach to research is helpful to activate your actor's imagination.

Valuable as research may be, your cast may not "own" the information until they turn it into their personal experience. Improvisation gives them this opportunity. You can structure for them situations, for example that explore the *News of the Day*, socially, politically, economically of a play's era that will have a visceral effect on them.

Even a relatively modern musical like Ragni and Rado's *Hair*, only several generations away from the Vietnam War, has become a period play, as its history and culture may feel separate from the young actors' experiences who will play these roles now.

Here is an example of an improv to serve as a quick history lesson for the actors to identify with their characters.

In *Hair*, we have a youth culture protesting what they consider an unjust war, in which they believe their country should not be involved. They protest against their president, Lyndon Johnson, the industrial-military complex, and the daily arrival at home of dead U.S. soldiers in body bags. These young, college-age men we see are vulnerable; as their numbers come up, they will be drafted.

I would suggest an improv for the cast that could strengthen both the stakes of their situation and the opposition they face from Americans who support the war, a group President Nixon will later call, "the silent majority," but who weren't all that silent.

Divide the cast into two groups. The first will be the "tribe," as the playwrights refer to the young people who are here in the East Village of New

York City conducting an informational session on the fallacy of the war, they call a teach-in.

The second group are spectators in the park who are not in the text, but will help offer the "tribe" the motivation they require to fire up their rebellion. These onlookers are ordinary, middle-class people of varying ages who have come, perhaps out of curiosity, to hear what these oddly dressed hippies have to say. The event soon turns into street theatre.

As the tribe becomes more vocal in their arguments to end the war, the spectator group becomes more agitated. One "silent majority" character might become vocal as he blurts out something like, "It's your patriotic duty to fight for your country." Tension builds between the two groups. A tribe character could take out his draft card saying, "This is what I think of the government", and he lights a match to it. Another bystander might respond, "I have a brother in the army in Vietnam." A tribe member restrains another comrade who starts to respond. The tribe might then break out into the chant: "Hey, hey, L.B.J. How many kids did you kill today?"

These are only suggestions to ignite the improv. You would counsel them to work toward, but avoid any actual physical violence.

Because all the characters in *Hair* share an anti-war point of view, it could be valuable to repeat this improv with some different circumstances, reversing the casting so each actor could experience the pro- and anti-war points of view.

Exercise #5
Analogous Situation

This kind of improv is geared to help the actors relate more fully to highly-charged situations in their play. It will likely come later in the rehearsal process in polishing rehearsals, when there is an emphasis on deepening the actor's emotional commitment. *Analogs situations* are those that are related to or similar to those in the text. They will be of value when an actor is having a problem, if their creativity shuts down and frustration follows. This often happens when actors have difficulty in believing in major events in the plot, which they have neither experienced nor can imaginatively identify with.

Assume your actor is playing the role of Lopakhin, the Russian merchant born a serf on the fabled Ranevskaya estate in Anton Chekhov's, *The Cherry Orchard*. Now wealthy, Lopakhin has purchased the Ranevskaya home and orchards. For some time, he has been courting Madame Ranevshaya's adopted daughter, Varya. It is assumed that a marriage will soon take place.

As the family is about to depart from their former estate, Lyubov assures Lopakhin that Varya loves him, and that he should propose now. He agrees. The mother practically pushes the eager daughter into the room to greet him.

It is at this moment in the script where our actor playing Lopakhin runs into trouble. He tells his director, "I don't understand this scene. I love the girl. I plan to propose and then I stammer and stall, talk of trifles like the weather, and rather than ask her to marry me, I make a quick excuse to leave and dash out the door." The coaching director, aware of the values of working with analogous situations says, "let's improv this scene in another time and place." He tells his actor; you are a modern-day "Construction worker. You are bright and ambitious, but a high school dropout. You plan to marry the educated daughter of a real estate mogul. "Stop!" says the now inspired actor, "I get it." "Of course, you do," says the director. "You understand the social and economic issues." "Yes," says the actor, "Now I understand my being born a serf on this estate, overwhelms me with feelings of low status and insecurity, and I feel unworthy of her."

The actors are anxious to rehearse the scene again. The director, however, urges them to first improv the socio-economic scenario that was described. The actors take on the roles, Lopakhin as a construction worker and Varya as a girl from the wealthy real estate family. The improv grows in reality as our actor playing Lopakhin now experiences the hesitancy, feels the hurt, and ponders the consequences of this marriage. "Cut," says the director. "Excellent, now let's return to the text Chekhov wrote." Such a substitution improv serves, to demonstrate the power inherent in working in rehearsals with *analogs situations*.

Exercise #6
Find the Metaphor

While improv is particularly suited to solving individual acting problems, it can be helpful as well in leading a cast to discover a play's overall theme or *super-objective*, Stanislavski's term for the major goal the protagonist is striving to achieve.

Let us take Samuel Beckett's classic, *Waiting for Godot*. This play, set the parameters for the *theatre of the absurd* dealing with characters who lack purpose and are trapped in what seems to them a meaningless universe. Two tramps, Didi and Gogo, have lost any sense of rational reasoning, if indeed they ever possessed any.

Consequently, they are caught up in a series of repetitive patterns of behavior from their past which previously might have held meaning, but now come as automatic responses. Their lives are a series of expectations that come to nothing. Each day they re-live yesterday's actions of expecting the arrival of a Mr. Godot whom they assume will offer them meaning, direction, or perhaps even salvation in their empty lives.

Each night, Godot fails to arrive, at which point the two tramps vow to leave immediately, but instead stand perfectly still. The text contains a series of attempted actions by Didi and Gogo that always result in inaction. As the director, you might help your actors arrive at their *super-objective* verb that might be described as: "To escape imprisonment from a hostile universe, where we repeat futile tasks."

In an improv, you then suggest for the actors that they are in the environment of the play surrounded by, in Beckett phrase, "all the dead leaves,"

Didi and Gogo will be split, standing downstage right and left. Ask them both to pick up a handful of "leaves", smoothing them out to make a neat pile in the palm of their hands. (Small packets of paper can serve as props or they may mime the actions.) They should then coordinate their movements to mirror each other. With their "leaves" in hand, they should counter cross the stage at the same time, arriving at the position where the other stood previously and place their leaves in a pile there. They should begin again to pick up leaves and continue to execute these redundant actions for several minutes, until you judge your actors have experienced extreme boredom.

After this silent improv, hopefully they are now in touch with the essence of the play. They have had a taste, in action, of the same gratuitous boredom and sense of entrapment in a seemingly senseless universe that Didi and Gogo experience. They should immediately return to playing the scene.

In your early rehearsal improvs that search for metaphors with appropriate physical actions that can aid your actors in experiencing the heart of the play's thematic meaning, can be valuable for your actors.

Exercise #7

Alter Ego

There are times in rehearsals when fatigue sets in, energy drops and a degree of frustration can descend over the work. The *Alter Ego* improv can be a strong antidote. This exercise, unlike most others here, offers an incongruity that may initially lead to laughter, but can provide a solution to scenes where a character conflicts with themselves, having difficulty making a decision based on possible alternatives.

In much of Shakespeare, such problems and their probable outcomes are written into the text. We call it soliloquy. Hamlet talks out loud to himself or his real or imagined audience in "to be or not to be." He debates the choice of suicide versus continued life; He concludes, "that the dread of something after death…makes us bear those ills we have, than fly to other we know not of." He has made the choice to embrace living through verbally debating the alternatives and making a decision that he shares with the audience.

More often in modern drama the character's dilemma is deeply buried, not explicit, but subtextual. This *Alter Ego* improv explores arguments between characters who are struggling with inner conflicting choices.

To solve this obstacle, select two actors not in a two-character scene, who will serve as the respective *Alter Egos* of each actor in it. They will voice a contrary solution to each of the character's problems. In this manner, a debate is created whereby, with another voice added, both sides of the character's problem will be heard; the *alter ego* who shadows behind, following his other self, offers an opposing argument. If, for instance, a weight-conscious character in a comedy scene says, "I'm so hungry. I could eat a horse," her alter ego actor might respond, "You might have a salad instead." *Alter Ego* is a valuable device for the actor to let their character explore various outcomes to their problems with an inner voice verbalizing a different course of action.

In strong, dramatic writing in a two-character scene, each actor will have opposing intentions, thus the value of *Alter Ego* characters is to expand through their arguments a greater range of possible outcomes.

The potential for a near brawl of opposing ideas exists in this exercise. This improv can shake loose a static scene and empower it with new life, as well as possibly offering a comic potential that you may not have considered.

Encourage your actors to physicalize the improv. The gentler the nudges, shoves, and playfully pushes the alter ego actor inflicts on their conflicted other-self, the more comedic the improv, and the more dynamic the results become.

To illustrate, let's looks at Romeo and Juliet in a scene where dire consequences present themselves through the characters struggle with their opposing needs. In Act III, Scene V of *Romeo and Juliet*, the two young lovers who have been secretly married have just spent their first night together. Romeo has been banished for the murder of Tybalt and must flee from Verona; Juliet makes a passionate plea for him to stay longer. She says she heard the cry of the nightingale, a bird that sings only in darkness, while Romeo is certain he has heard the lark, "the herald of the morn." He argues it is not safe to stay. Within a few lines, however, motivated by their passionate love, they will reverse their positions. Romeo declares, "I have more care to stay than will to go. Come death and welcome! Juliet wills it so…Let's talk it is not day." Juliet immediately contradicts him. "It is, it is! Hi hence, be gone away. It is the lark that sings so out of tune."

Characters vacillating between highly consequential opposing choices create powerful drama. By asking the two actors who are the alter egos to verbalize and argue the other side of the issue with their other self, new choices can strengthen the scene when they return to it after the improv. As the alter egos prolong the argument, the actors will find more motivation to strengthen their reversal of positions, discover the scene's transitions and explore the subtext more deeply. A further major contribution can be the actor's discovery of the humor waiting to be found.

Exercise #8
What Just Happened?

Coaching directors often ask actors just before their entrance, "What was your character's moment before?" The reason for the question is to urge them to make basic choices as to the specific place their character is coming from, what has just happened to them and what do they need now from the other characters?

What happens, however, if actors caught up in their characters' immediate detail miss the big picture? What if they are so self-absorbed in their moment-to-moment behavior that they lose touch with a crucial action that will affect their characters' lives? I am referring to an arc of events in the play's story that may occur while their character is offstage, or between the acts as time passes in the plot. Or it may be an event that is happening elsewhere simultaneously while there is a different stage action.

This *what just happened* event may be of such importance that it requires more attention than just a reminder from the director. It may be a moment that needs to be experienced by your cast, physically and emotionally through improv.

I am suggesting that playwrights are prone to bury their plots. Especially in modern drama there is the tendency for significant events to lie under the surface. I spoke in the last chapter of the *subtext* often being more important than the surface dialogue. Your cast will profit from the tool of improv to explore essential events that can so easily be overlooked.

Let us again examine Chekhov's *The Cherry Orchard* in a crucial moment near the end of Act III. It is the day of the family's estate auction. This seems far from the concerns of the onstage action where the characters are in the midst of a party.

Ranevskya, the estate owner, has thrown a ball replete with the presence of the local orchestra. That she is penniless seems of no consequence to her. The simultaneous offstage actions concern her brother Gayev and the wealthy merchant Lopakhin who are at the auction where they will bid on the estate. The moment we will examine is the actual sale of it, which we don't see on stage. What we do see is their return home from it. Lopakhin enters first and a moment later, Gayev neither makes any mention of where they have been.

Lopakhin endures a comic accident. His presumed fiancé Varya has mistaken him for a bothersome servant and banged him over the head with a cane. His only response is "thank you kindly." Gayev's first words to the old servant, Firs, are, "Here take, take these anchovies, Kerch herrings…I haven't eaten all day." The scene is not about the merchant's benign acceptance of being smacked or of the brother's hunger. If your actors were to look no further, they would miss the major action of the play, as its crisis has just occurred *offstage*. The estate had been sold; Lopakhin is the elated new owner and Gayev the dejected former one. This action will be made clear as the act progresses, but Chekhov had a different intent.

The awareness of this situation, change of ownership, must be played and communicated on the entrance of Lopakhin and Gayev through their subtext and body language so it is clear to all the other characters at the party and the audience as well.

In an improvisation, which should precede rehearsals of this scene, the end of the auction should be played with the entire cast watching it. Ask Gayev and Lopakhin to spontaneously create the moments they share just after the auctioneer's gavel falls, signifying the transfer of the ancestral property to Lopakhin.

Have those actors explore their long relationships with one another based on rich possibilities like guilt, resentment, and perhaps even affection that may surface between them. This will not only enrich the actors with their entrance upon returning home, but their entire stage life together. With this crucial event dramatized as an improv, all the actors will better understand the central issue of the text and will realize the need to consider acting choices concerning the consequences of the ultimate ownership of the estate from the beginning of the play.

Discussions of character intentions and the subtext of a scene are essential. Sometimes, however, the complexities of issues in a play get so distanced from the moment they occur that improvisation is the most effective means to achieve clarity for the actors.

Exercise #9
Classic Film Comedy

As rehearsals progress, one of your major roles as a coaching director is to continue to inspire your actors to find new layers of reality in their acting. This will be the work of later polishing rehearsals when the company has made a series of basic discoveries about their characters and have achieved an acceptable level of belief in them.

At this point, some directors will advise their actors to "set it" and move on to new material. That phrase is always dangerous. It tends to inhibit further exploration and growth. As a coaching director, you need to consistently encourage your actors to reach new heights, to keep exploring different aspects of their characters. For the director to give even tacit consent that final work has been achieved on a portion of the play before the last rehearsal is to encourage your actors to become complacent in their roles.

Improvisation in later rehearsals is a way of encouraging them to keep searching for discoveries rather than freezing moments that may have yet to reach their full potential.

One powerful way to achieve this is to play topsy-turvy. That is, to ask your actors to work with choices opposite to the conventional expectations of a scene. If you are working on a serious drama that is progressing, but has yet to peak, explore the material in improv as a farce. If this sounds peculiar, consider the power of opposites. The discovery of a comic choice may be the key that drives the psychological validity of a dramatic moment. Shakespeare and Chekhov, among other great dramatists, show us that human beings can be both noble and buffoonish almost simultaneously.

The bishop puts on his miter, begins to ascend his alter, slips on a waxed step, takes a pratfall, gets up and regains his humanity, perhaps even enhances it. We call such a situation an incongruity and we laugh.

We will, however, likely feel a stronger empathy for the embarrassed bishop, as the serious and the absurd live side-by-side in us always.

Why sepárate them onstage? We should not and the best playwrights give actors ample opportunities to discover that.

Let us return to *The Cherry Orchard* and the wrenching scene of the proposal that still hasn't happened between Varya and the merchant Lopakhin. I discussed earlier this improv is for both actors to understand the strong obstacles blocking their relationship. When they return to the scene, you may be concerned that they are playing the problems of their different social class, versus romantic expectation so intensely, that some of the tension needs to be released to find other colors in the text.

Here is where experimenting with opposites comes into play. Ask your actors to improv the attempted proposal in the genre of, screwball comedy. Counsel them to drop all elements of serious drama; ask both actors to choose a comic film icon as their character. For example, how would Lopakhin behave if he entered the scene in the character of Charlie Chaplin? Then ask your Varya to take on the persona of Lucille Ball. Suggest to your actors they lose their dignity and play in a clownish style.

You should then ask your Lucy/Varya to be soulful and blubbering as she makes excuses for having come into the room. To cover her distress, she might frantically open a trunk, packed for the move, searching for imaginary objects to give Lopakhin time to get his courage to propose. In the course of attempting to be casual, while adjusting the trunk's lining that is loose, her ring gets caught there and in attempting to free it, she rips out the whole fabric. She was it up as if it were invisible, stuffs it in her pocket, looks up, and smiles at Lopakhin as she inadvertently slams the trunk shut on her hand. She explodes in comic pain in an ear-splitting Lucy type wail.

Lopakhin, as the ever-gallant Charlie Chaplin, crosses to console her, but stumbles and manages to nearly kick her in the head before he regains his balance. This results in further cries of anguish from Varya. He is distressed and can only think of the gentlemanly custom of tipping his derby hat to her, which she indignantly grabs and swats on the floor. As his nervous ticks overcome his good intentions, he flees the room in embarrassment. He fails to restrain his clumsiness and trips over the doorsill as he bows to her and stumbles out.

Over the top? Of course! It is the broadest, farce comedy. Should your actors' slapstick bits find their way into your finished production of *The Cherry Orchard*? Absolutely Not! After the high exuberance of this improv, you should suggest your actors return to rehearsing the text, playing it for the choices that were developing before this comic interlude. You should suggest to them, however, that they recall their characters' physical awkwardness, panic and vulnerability experienced in the improv. Ask them to work to get in touch with some of the human comedy that is universal in even the most serious life situations. Your production will be stronger as a result.

Finding the comic in the serious text and the serious in the comic, can lead your actors to new insights in their work. These exercises offer some of the many possibilities in which improvs can benefit your cast and your rehearsals process.

As a coaching director, you will be continually finding new applications for improvs throughout the entire rehearsal process. You may be pleased as well with time saved with quick solutions to problems through improvs. They have the advantage of immediately putting the actor's thoughts and impulses into action as they grow in risk-taking and spontaneity.

4

Exploratory Rehearsals

We move now to the coaching director's entire journey from your first rehearsal to opening night. We will work through the four phases of the process, exploratory rehearsals, blocking and interpreting, in-depth polishing rehearsals then final run-throughs and dresses.

You have arrived early at the rehearsal space in order to greet and congratulate your cast members as they enter. You communicate to them in a friendly, open and professional manner. When the cast is assembled, you move to the front of the group to offer a few thoughts before the first rehearsal begins.

What is needed here is your positive energy to continue building your casts enthusiasm and commitment to the work ahead together.

You might start by letting them know they are the cast you wished for and they are here because they earned their roles in competitive tryouts. It is most important to tell them that as a collaborative director, you want and need their input throughout the rehearsal process.

Identify yourself as a director-actor coach committed to guiding them as challenges arise in their roles. Inform your actors that you will lead them in new active approaches, using improvs, exercises, and games in the rehearsals ahead to achieve the strongest ensemble and quality of work possible and that work will start with a nontraditional first reading of the play.

I have often observed a particular problem occurring as rehearsals begin. The following is only a slightly exaggerated version of the *Deadly First Reading.*

The actors gather on a cold, dim stage, frequently with work lights that offer less than ample illumination. They sit on rickety folding chairs. The director commands them to read the text non-stop, the tone of this rehearsal is usually all too predictable.

As they begin, the actor's tensions mount dramatically. To compensate their anxieties, they most likely become over-competitive, feeling an urge to impress both the director and their peers. What follows is a forced performance. Rather than searching for understanding, the actors go for results. The consequences are, inauthentic emotions, minimal listening, negligent actor connection, and quite likely an emphasis on one-upmanship, rather than a search for their characters' needs. The following exercises will explore how the coaching director can guide actors through the first rehearsals and problems that may follow.

Exercise #1
The Spontaneous Impulse Reading

First, banish the grey atmosphere. If the rehearsal is on stage, be certain there is ample light. A brightly lit lounge or green room with comfortable seating may prove a better location. Arrange the furniture in a circular configuration so each cast member and the director can easily establish eye contact with one another. Help the company relax by conversing together for a while before the read begins.

You might ask the actors what appeals to them most about the play or what intrigues them about their characters. Then you break from tradition. The play will be read in its entirety, but not with the actors reading their roles!

Explain that this first encounter together should be an impulsive experience. That is, it should start spontaneously with any participant reading the first speech other than the actor cast in the role. Gender is arbitrary and a prescribed order of readers should be avoided so the reading is truly spontaneous.

An actor speaks when they feel the impulse. You will contribute as well, by reading when there is a hesitation. A spirited energy emerges from this process that releases the anxiety and tension associated with the first read. Rather than potential self-interest and competition, the actors enter into a cooperative exercise to keep the flow of the reading moving forward. Because of the spontaneity involved, premeditated readings of the text are eliminated.

The significant value in this unconventional approach is that each actor hears different voices speaking their words. They experience both the play and their role with new insight. The story emerges in this reading and the actors will begin to grasp character relationships rather than concentrating only on their lines.

After the reading, I suggest you postpone any presentation of interpretive or conceptual ideas until the next rehearsal when there will be more time to discuss them. You may, however, choose to have a brief discussion focused on what each actor learned about the play and/or their character as they listened to the other voices. Attempt to get a response from each actor in your company no matter how small their role.

If there is time remaining, introduce your next group exercise. This period of exploratory rehearsals ahead, is unique to the coaching director's strategy. The intent is three-fold: First, there is work on individual acting issues such as relaxation, sensory awareness, and concentration. Second, the goal is to begin to build a strong actor ensemble that works together seamlessly. Third, a textual exploration will be undertaken that probes into character background and relationships earlier and in more depth than the traditional rehearsal model. Present and past circumstances in the script are investigated through improvisations, games, and exercises.

Exercise #2

Sending the Spark

The cast, sitting in a circle, either on chairs or on the floor, join hands. A company member initiates the spark by squeezing the hand of the partner next to them. That actor repeats that action as they send the spark on, and the energy flows around the circle until it returns to the original sender, who starts a second round.

Now each participant varies the length and intensity of the squeeze from short to longer and soft to stronger. The intent is for all the actors to experience a sense of connection. They should concentrate to experience the squeeze as a current of electricity that flows through the entire cast.

While this is a tangible physical exercise, it is also a metaphor that represents the unity and interdependence of the group as they receive and send energy to one another. It can be performed in several minutes. If the spark catches fire with your actors, you can use it as a warm-up exercise as often as needed.

Exercise #3

The Designer's sparks

I would suggest the second rehearsal might contain several major objectives, first, being a presentation of your production concept. Many directors find it important in these early rehearsals to have a session in which they present to the cast their interpretation of the production. This is often followed by a question and answer session, a discussion of themes, the author's background, social and/or political relevance, among other issues of importance in the text. I have found it valuable to invite my design colleagues to this session to speak and particularly to show where they are at this moment in their design process.

The director and the designers have been collaborating for many weeks before this date. They have worked to find common ground so each production element, set, costumes, lights, and sound communicate the same central ideas in the script chosen by the director as their production concept. The director is the unifier of the production. It is of considerable importance to bring the design staff and the director together for a joint presentation so the actors can see their visualizations and the challenges, everyone is working on together. The actors will realize they must strive in their characters to strengthen the overall production concept.

The scenic designer will likely bring a cardboard scale model of the set and perhaps a color rendering as well. These tools provide essential information for the cast. Actors can visualize the production's three-dimensional acting spaces and their characters within them. They will know the location of entrances and exits, suggested furniture arrangements, and a variety of acting areas and levels within the set. Give them a moment to memorize or sketch their rough ground plan. This can save time and confusion later.

A complete lighting design traditionally arrives later in the production process, but the designer may suggest his initial ideas to the company. They can help the actors to envision their roles by describing the varying moods and atmospheres of light, as the play progresses.

The costume designer, likewise, will be an immense aid as they show costume plates and fabric swatches of the character's clothes. Actors seeing what they will wear in the production is a powerful stimulus for their imagination. It may allow them to gather some mock-up clothes they might wear during rehearsals.

The director's conceptual presentation should precede the visuals of the designers. The essential purpose of this session is to demonstrate that the director and their fellow artists have a unified view of the production and are asking the actors to join them in that vision.

You are ready now to begin one of the major goals of these exploratory rehearsals. That is, the use of improvisation as a tool for your actors to better understand and interpret the text.

Because of its importance, I devoted the last chapter to exploring its various possibilities in detail; I suggested improvisation be used frequently in these early rehearsals. Using the play as your single source, you need to develop a series of situations of the play's given circumstances in the present and past time of the story, as discussed in the last chapter. The length of each improv should be limited to several minutes. Your entire cast will either act or serve as a constructive audience. You will then lead a discussion to evaluate, not their acting skills, but rather an analysis of what the improvisation revealed concerning the play's events and the character's relationships to one another.

As you begin a group discussion at the end of each improv, focus on what everyone saw and learned about the major events in that episode. Ask the participating actors what they experienced as their characters, and their relationships with their partners.

As you open up the evaluation to the group, ask about the performer's accuracy of the playwright's *given circumstances*. Did the actors deal with the facts of the play accurately? Do not hesitate to clear up information your cast may have missed or interpreted incorrectly.

Ask the non-performing cast members, what they saw or heard, during the improv, or noticed any choices from the actors that might influence their character's relationships. These improvisations can offer your actors a new level of understanding of the play's structure, characters, and themes; providing valuable information before rehearsals move forward. The next two exercises deal with the problem of excessive actor muscular tension and how it may be eliminated with relaxation imagery exercises.

Exercise #3

Melt Down

Here is a preparation exercise to enable your actors to banish the tensions of their day and prepare for the rehearsal ahead. On stage or in a large room ask them to find a private space and lie flat on the floor. They should close their eyes as you offer the following fantasy circumstances:

Imagine yourself on a soft vinyl floor in a comfortable kitchen. It is as if you are a cube of frozen butter on that floor. You retain your own identity, only your exterior has changed. Take a moment to visualize your shape and texture. Now, be aware that a ceiling heater has been turned on and hot air circulates around you. Resist the warmth as long as you can. At first, you prefer your rigid state, but the warmth is increasingly seductive. Feel, despite your resistance, you are transforming into another entity. You are slowly melting into a liquid state.

Once the initial thaw has begun, you soon experience the languorous, flowing energy of your new condition. You are still yourself with all your faculties, but now possessing a new elasticity and mobility. You are no longer bound, but are free to float, flow, or glide with ease. Take the time you need to sense your movement in space and your change in physical condition. Now open your eyes slowly. Holding onto your new awareness, very slowly rise and move about the acting space. You are now prepared to enter into a productive rehearsal.

Tension is the actor's enemy. The director needs to help the company shed the rigidities in their bodies, that block the freedom of their acting impulses which need to be open and available to the play and their partners.

The most effective manner for the actor to conquer this problem is to experience in their bodies any excessive tension, overcome it by releasing muscular tightness and experience complete bodily freedom. Suggest to your actors the analogy that their bodies should be free like an untangled hose, that when turned on gives forth a powerful, full flowing stream of water. If that hose gets knotted, it loses its power and sputters out only weak drops of moisture. Likewise, when there are knots of tension anywhere in the actor's body, their energy stream, their power, is blocked. They are physically inhibited from delivering the performance they strive to achieve. The director must assist each member of their cast when needed to release tension and help them achieve the level of relaxation required for their optimal performance.

Exercise #5
Tension and Release

Ask your actors to remove their shoes and find their individual space to spread their feet slightly and achieve a wide base. The purpose here is to move from the feet up, to the top of their head, experiencing a sense of extreme tension. Then, slowly release it to achieve relaxation.

Talk to your actors through this exercise. Ask them to experience wet cement under their feet that quickly dries, securing them to the floor. This cement is then applied up to their ankles and those muscles lock in rigidity. The cement now travels up to both knees, a sense of encasement is beginning to occur. Request the group to imagine that the wet cement comes up both legs to their hips and then encircles their waist. It dries instantly; half their body is now immobile while the other half is completely free. Ask them to get in touch with the juxtaposition of total lower immobility and upper freedom. They should swing their arms and slowly roll their head as they go limp to the waist, as if they were a rag doll.

Ask them now to bring their head to an upright position. The rigidity continues. Suggest your men feel a sense of heavy chainmail armor from their neck to waist that will force them to tense those muscle groups. For the women, offer an image, that they are underdressed in an elaborate 19th-century corset and that an imaginary hand is tying and tightening all the strings.

Ask the actors now to place their arms in front of them, palms out with fingers spread, and push a wheelbarrow full of bricks uphill with all their strength. Let the tension grow from the neck to the head. They should then open their mouths, bite down hard on an imaginary apple and hold this total state of tension for approximately ten seconds.

Now, ask them to slowly release from head to toes. First, let them experience their head, heavy as a bowling ball, begin to gradually pull them downward. Ask them to open their mouths, attempt to yawn, and vocalize that sound. For the women, all the straps and strings of their corset break loose and the inhibiting garment falls off. Likewise, the men's chainmail shatters and falls to the ground in pieces. Ask the actors to feel the complete freedom of their upper bodies while from waist to feet they remain encased in concrete.

Now, the remaining cement slowly breaks. The actors feel the enormous release of the lower body, which responds to gravity, is slowly pulling them to the ground. Carefully, breaking their fall to the floor in slow motion, the actors land in a fetal position, lying still for a long moment. They should have now gotten in touch with total relaxation and can reflect on the harmful state of tension versus the feeling of total ease when released from it. After an appropriate moment, ask them to very slowly sit up on the floor, holding on to their newfound relaxation.

These next two exercises may be performed in a brief amount of time. Their results will be reflected in your finished production as they are opportunities for your entire cast to bond together. They are designed to build acceptance, trust, and team spirit, which is essential in an ensemble production.

Exercise #6
The Silent Gift

The cast breaks into couples. Each pair sits on the floor or in chairs facing each other. They begin a silent dialogue as they look directly into their partner's eyes. Ask them to discover something about the other they didn't know before, her eye color, or the contour of his eyebrows. The actors should have a positive unspoken dialogue with each other. They might be thinking these words, "Working with you in this company is special; it is like receiving a gift."

One partner then proceeds to engage in that specific action. Silently the actor presents a gift to their partner of a real physical object that is on their person, perhaps a ring, a comb, or an article of clothing such as a sweater or a shoe. The partner accepts the gift with non-verbal thanks. They then reverse the procedure. At the end of this encounter, the "gifts" are returned and the actors move onto another cast member until presents have been exchanged among the entire ensemble. They then share a handshake or a hug all around to conclude the experience.

Exercise #7
Living Entities

Ask all the characters who are sympathetic to one another in the play to link their arms together and form a single-file line, close their eyes, and explore the thought that they are one separate living person. Then, ask for the formation of a second group whose characters are in opposition to the other.

For example, in *West Side Story* you would ask the Shark gang to form one line and their rivals the Jets the other. You are requesting those characters with similar values, supportive of one another, to band together. Urge your actors to experience this kinetically.

Both groups, now separated in their own space, begin to slowly move in the same direction as one body. Each actor must attempt to avoid individually influencing another in terms of a movement impulse. The goal is for the actors to receive rather than send energy. Each member attempts to discover the intentions of their overall group. Allow them several minutes to experiment with synchronized movement, forward, backward, and laterally; any impulse that continues to bind them together.

Now ask the two groups to seek each other out. As they enter the other's territorial space, they may even collide with one another. If there is a bodily connection between them, one group should retreat. The energy between the two should not be so much an explosion of violence as it is, apprehension and tension.

The exercise should conclude with each entity in their own space reinforcing their solidarity through their synchronized breath and movement. The exercise builds the actor's sense of responsibility to each other and their consequent feelings of trust within their group. You may initially wish to use only the one sympathetic character group and add the antagonist unit in later rehearsals, or omit them if it doesn't fit the needs of your script.

Exercise #8
Character Interviews

Seated around a table where intimacy, eye contact, and comfort can easily be achieved, the coaching director begins an essential questioning process aimed at the actors gaining insight into their characters. In this exercise the entire cast will play their characters in improvisational responses about their lives.

You, the director, will assume a character as well. You will be the *Interviewer* in a T.V. studio who will chair this "reality show." The director as a journalist is an apt analogy of your work at this stage of rehearsal. The "Elementary W's", who, what, where, when, and why, which were explored in improvisations, continue here as you inquire about a series of events in the characters past and present life. The actors will respond in the first person. The sooner they say "I", the faster their imagination will transport them into action.

Some directors request that their actors write character sketches, biographies, or diaries about their characters' lives. This can be valuable for actors who gain knowledge best by recording their thoughts on paper. For others, however, the formal procedures of writing their impressions may be stifling and can be a sterile intellectualization rather than a spontaneous discovery about their character.

An oral discussion seems the better approach for the entire cast together who all need a common base of information of the play's circumstances, at this stage of rehearsals.

As the *Interviewer*, you will probe the characters with questions that will allow them to define themselves in detail. The first questions might deal with vital statistics. What is your approximate age and weight? How is your general health and level of vitality? You would then progress to the character's biography with questions about their childhood continuing to the present. What is your educational background, your hobbies, professional duties, social life, and style of dress?

Questions should then begin to open up the more psychological and sociological aspects of their character. What is your environment like? How does it influence your life choices? What is your outlook on life? How would you define your self-concept? How might you behave under specific emotionally stressful situations?

When using *Character Interviews,* you, have the control to ask about the various character's conflicting opinions. If, for instance, you were interviewing the Loman family of, *Death of a Salesman*, and Willy Loman said, "I am a devoted father and loving husband." As an alert *Interviewer*, you would call on his son, Biff, to confirm or deny that assertion. He might heatedly reply, "You are a phony and a liar. I know about your affair with the women in Boston."

As the actors hear more details of each other's backgrounds they will agree or debate, sometimes passionately, about their relationships with one another. A kind of family counseling session can occur with this experience.

You may raise questions as a therapist might, withholding judgment. The more incisive and specific your questions, the greater the potential for the actor's discoveries. It may take a full rehearsal to complete the *Interviewer's* questions for each character. You will find it time well spent.

Exercise #9
Show Me

This exercise is a logical extension of *Character Interviews*. Sometimes the information the actors contribute verbally, while of interest, is not always essential. There is frequently a tendency for actors to intellectualize their character's circumstances. You may need to help them get out of their heads and physicalize their characters.

The gifted American director, Elia Kazan, spoke a gem of wisdom when he said, "The art of directing is turning psychology into behavior." Behavior is created in the actor's physical actions, what the characters do and how they do it. Combing one's hair, sipping a drink, buckling a belt or putting on boots are common physical actions, but the *manner* in which an actor does them, will reveal character. They are turning narrative into behavior.

If the actor playing Lennie in, *Of Mice and Men,* tells you he is 5'10", has a protruding stomach, and walks with a slight hitch in his gait, it's time to say, "Show me." Rather than encouraging a generalized discussion, ask your actor to get to their feet and experience that behavior. Guide them along the way using four principles.

First, ask them where their *lead* is? That is what part of their body dominates when they move in space. What body feature is most prominent? I am referring to a center of gravity, as we might discover it in a piece of sculpture. Lennie suggested that it was his stomach. Can he physicalize that idea? He should attempt now. Ask him to move with a feeling of excess body weight in his stomach. It should protrude outward and *lead* him. It should catch a bystander's eye when he first sees Lennie.

Encourage your actors to experiment with these major body leads of head, heart, stomach, and groin. When your actors choose a specific center and physicalize it, they begin to build a character different from themselves. The Russian actor/teacher, Michael Chekhov, said that any part of the actor's body may be used as a lead. If you or your actors have not previously been introduced to this process, it may appear a bit strange. With brief experimentation, however, you will find it quite startling how quickly the actor's sense of their character can be changed or enhanced by creating an appropriate physical center. A bold specific physical lead can jumpstart a characterization.

The second element, *tempo*, is the quickest technique to transform the actor. They ask themselves, how does the temperament or health of my character cause me to move slower or faster than I do? Their opportunity for characterization will be greater if they can choose the opposite of their life tempo.

The third element is *force*. What is the intensity of the character in their gestures and the handling of objects? With what degree of energy does Lenny pet a mouse? How "delicately" versus how "intensely"? Does a character, in order to make a point, pound on a table with his fist or glide over it with their open hand?

Finally, your actors should consider *space*. The physical impression of the actor's body changes dramatically by the amount of *space* their character occupies. Again, this is an example of psychology revealed in physical actions, consider introverts and extroverts. A shy, awkward character may tend to retreat in *space*. In stressful situations a character may almost shrink, physically turning inward; they might seem to close off as their feet come closer together and their arms across their chest.

The extrovert, on the other hand, may extend themselves in *space*. They conquer it. With a broad base, their head and upper body move forward as they sprawl and luxuriate on a couch. I offer broad visual stereotypes here to illustrate the principle. Your actors can also use space more subtly in their characterization.

In moments of stress a character may find the courage to act contrary to their basic character leads. The previously weak victim stands up for themselves and becomes more expansive. The blustering bully retreats in their *space* when a stronger character calls their bluff. Your actors should consider how their character's physicality in *space* might change through the progression of the play.

These physical choices can make profound differences in characterization.

So, if your actors need help when you say *Show Me*, suggest they concentrate on these four physical techniques of *lead, tempo, force,* and *space* which can immediately go to work on their imaginations and produce strong results.

You may work with other elements as well. Inanimate images are likewise useful. Ask your actors to imagine objects that could resemble aspects of their characters and have them playfully experiment with them physically.

Challenge your actors by asking them, "If you were a piece of furniture, a flower, season of the year, a toy, music, house, type of transportation, color, or household implement, how would you move and speak?? Any of these or other images you might suggest in these exploratory rehearsals can spark your actors' imaginations to create choices that may be both original and appropriate to their characters. There is power in *Show Me*.

Exercise #10
Treasure Hunt

This exercise continues in the same vein challenging actors to explore new and different avenues of developing a character. In the first week of rehearsal, request that your actors embark on a personal *treasure hunt*, a journey in search of an essence for their characters. An essence is an analogy. Finding something in an inorganic object or animal that is so strikingly similar to the character's behavior, that by incorporating it in their choices helps create a highly original characterization.

In this exercise the actor will go on an actual search to discover their character's essence, which could reveal an inward nature of their character. Ask your actors to seek out a place where this inspiration might occur. For example, it could be a fine art museum, a music library, a zoo, an antique store or a thrift shop. This quest may result in discovering the character's essence based on a painting, a musical selection, an animal, an object, or a piece of clothing. They may need to journey to several locations before they find it. You should set a deadline for the actor to demonstrate it when you will be off-book for the first unit of the play.

You should encourage your actors once they have discovered an essence to observe it in detail. They should spend about half an hour in observation and sensory examination of it; they may need to return to its location for further study.

You will ask them to speak several lines of their dialog as they move across the stage, working to achieve the character's essence that was observed, imagined, and practiced. It will hopefully offer fresh, creative choices for them.

When the actors perform this exercise in rehearsal, it should be a moment between them and the director only. This provides you more freedom to critique what you saw. You should evaluate the appropriateness of your actor's essence choice with a recommendation to apply it in the rehearsal ahead or search further. In either case, you should be encouraging. These individual critiques can be accomplished in several minutes and should be scheduled before the group rehearsal. *Treasure Hunt* helps establish the actor's mindset that the search for their character continues throughout rehearsals.

These exploratory sessions of improvisations, relaxation, creating an ensemble, actor connection, and character development will be the shortest of the four major sections of rehearsals on the production. These goals may be introduced in approximately four to six rehearsals.

Exercise #11

The Actors Journal

Before we conclude this introduction to the many possibilities here for your actors to begin to discover their creative potential, I suggest you then ask them to commit to an outside of the rehearsal project. It is a personal journal that will chronicle their journey throughout the rehearsal process. There should be a daily entry of the actor's challenges, experiments, frustrations, but certainly great pleasure in problem-solving and making discoveries. Further, it will avoid a familiar actor trap. Too often, actors lured by the convenience of the compact acting edition of their play, begin writing. In addition to their blocking, they add their thoughts on script analysis, character discoveries, backstory, and subtext. Soon all the available limited space is consumed and despite their attempt at near-microscopic handwriting, it becomes impossible to decipher. To avoid illegible scripts, your actors should create a separate diary size journal, that will have the same numbering as their acting edition scripts. Urge your actors to set aside time for daily entries in this journal. They can, for example, study the next scene(s) to be worked in the rehearsal ahead and make ongoing preparation on their roles. They should include thoughts, questions and new choices to be explored. Let us examine now some important discoveries your actors can make about their characters in this journal homework.

Exercise 12

Me/My Character

For this exercise, your actors should create two personality trait profiles; one of themselves and the other of their character. This will give them an instant picture of the similarities and the differences that exist between themselves and their character. They should draw a line down the center of the page of their journal from the top to bottom. On the top left side, they will write *Me*, and on the top right side, they write their character's name. Ask them to list of all the most recognizable personality traits they can discover demonstrated by their character's actions in the play. Then, they should do a self-analysis and list as many as possible of their personality traits, both positive and negative. With these two lists, "Me" and "My character" they have created their own valuable acting exercise.

Let me illustrate with an example of a well-known actor's use of this process. Famed actor, Gregory Peck, next to each beat of dialogue in his scripts, wrote, "Acting" or "No Acting". At first glance, it might appear that Mr. Peck had an overly casual approach to his career. The term "No Acting" was likely intended not as an invitation to disregard that portion of the text, but rather that he recognized himself in these passages and he would deal with them differently. Peck had been trained by famed acting teacher, Sanford Meisner, and he understood the value of self-use. That is, the actors using their feelings and experiences in developing a character.

"Me" traits are those aspects of the actor's personality shared with the character. They will prove to be valuable triggers for the actor to get in touch with their feelings and emotions that are analogous to those in their role.

For example, in a scene about a young man speaking to his girlfriend in a hasty, impulsive manner, that upsets her, the actor will search their behavior for a moment and choose two of their personality traits, that have caused them trouble in their relationships. They identify them as impetuosity and bluntness. They are flooded with images of embarrassing personal recollections that can be useful, as they transfer them to their character.

As your actors concentrate on these traits in a sense memory experience of a time, place, the people present, and their *physical condition,* they will re-experience the event.

This is the essence of the actor's self-use work. "Me" choices may be among your actors most authentic performance moments. Now, what about the other side of the equation, the textual character? Your actors here face the challenge of engaging in creative dreaming. They must now work to understand what it would be like behaving differently than their accustomed behavior.

Personality traits, they might vigorously avoid in everyday life, must now, not only be accepted, but embraced.

It is not the actor's personal life but the playwright's story and the words of their character that will require their most concentrated focus. They will work with both subjective imagination and objective analysis. They will make the world of the play their own world through their imagination and inner imagery.

Your actors will choose a specific character trait in each beat of the text that offers major clues in discovering the strongest *psychological action.* As your actors progress in rehearsals with their preparation work, they will choose one or more-character traits for each crucial transition of the script. Let us say they have selected three personality traits: Resolute, Intolerance, and Stubbornness. The actor imagines the mix of textual circumstances with the traits, and chooses the verb to dominate. Gathering diverse personality traits offers greater range and color to the actor's character. They should think in terms of progression and contrast. The best playwrights have written these shifts of moods from sunny to stormy weather as a character's journey progresses.

Suggest to your actors, that in choosing their traits, they should work for subtle character changes as they move *beat* to *beat*. They should as well, find some different aspects of behavior on each new entrance. This process is sometimes referred to as, "peeling the onion", that is continuing to reveal a different layer of their character's skin. Here is a list of some major personality traits that can be helpful for your actors. Feel free to expand or abridge them to fit their needs.

Sensitivity	Self esteem	Leadership	Responsiveness
Consideration	Humor	Wit	Idealism
Imagination	Intuition	Tolerance	Intolerance
Dominant	Resolute	Restlessness	Stubbornness
Ambitious	Generosity	Impetuosity	Need to be noticed
Analytical	Courageous	Intelligence	Concentration
Depression	Bluntness	Tactful	Optimistic

Suggest to your actors that their characters will experience each trait in varying degrees. They may wish to rate them as low, medium, or high.

This exercise will build a strong motivation for your actors. as they begin their character journal, and continue to make daily comments on their discoveries and preparations for rehearsals ahead. The actors understanding of how they are similar to their character and how they are different, is an important ingredient for their success in a role.

Exercise #13
Dream Through

The goal of this exercise is to allow your actors to take an imaginary trip through their entire role. Ask the cast to lie on the floor, ideally in a carpeted comfortable space. They should close their eyes and first think of the time when the action of the play takes place. Then, have them begin to visualize where they are. If it is in an interior space, they should see the room, the furniture, and the major objects that surround them. If outdoors, have them picture the environment in detail.

They should then place themselves in the plays season of the year. If inside, ask them to look out a window, see the weather and have a sensory reaction to it. What is the time of day, how might it affect their mood? Now, request they visualize how they are dressed and what accessories, if any, they are wearing.

Next, in their imagination only, they should rise, move about and interact in their environment. Ask them to execute a specific physical activity they do in the play like setting a table or chopping wood. As they perform the action in their mind, they should be aware of the body center with which they are leading.

Is their character's rhythm faster or slower than their own? As the actors visualize themselves in various physical actions, they should determine the degree to which their character either extends themselves aggressively in space or submissively retreats.

Now, they should choose a scene of conflict in the play where they are involved in a dispute with another character. What do they need to get from them? Visualize what stands in the way of getting it. They should see themselves struggling to achieve it. If they do not succeed, they should feel the humiliation or regret. If they win, they should experience a sense of power and pleasure in their victory. Give your actors time to visualize and work through these experiences.

Next, request them to choose an emotional event or crisis in the script where they experience anxiety, anger, fear, happiness, or love. Ask them to get in touch with an incident in their own life that is close to that experience.

Request your actors now, to envision their character at the end of the play. Ask them, finally, if they can discover any differences in their character from when their story began. How have they changed through their journey?

5

Discussion To Improv To Action To Blocking

There may be a temptation for you to prolong your exploratory rehearsals because they are both productive and enjoyable for the actors, but you need to move on to the next phase of the work after three to five days of exploration. Some of the more productive exercises that have resulted in breakthroughs for your actors and others that time did not permit you to investigate, may be revisited or explored in later rehearsals.

We move now to the second major stage of our work, blocking the production. As I suggested in the first chapter, the coaching director's approach to staging offers the boldest departure from traditional rehearsal procedures. It moves from director-centered blocking to collaborative staging in which the director and actors work together to block the play. While this is the choice of many contemporary directors, it is not yet common practice. The coaching director's method of blocking involves a five-step procedure that saves rehearsal time, gives actors the information they need in a more logical sequence, and builds cast morale.

I need to discuss two issues before we begin to examine this approach. The first is a resistance to change directing procedures based on the dominance of the *instructional director* in the long history of the theatre. The second is a need to discuss the importance of the play's ground plan and how it influences and to a degree controls a play's staging.

When contrasted with the long-documented history of Western drama from approximately 534 B.C.E., it is not until the 19th century that we have the name of a single professional whose only responsibility was working with actors. Before that time, it was the duty of the playwright, or if he was not present or willing to serve, the leading actor, often the manager of the theatre company, to assure the basic directorial needs.

The present-day director, when observed through twenty-five centuries of theatre history, is a relatively new arrival on the theatre scene. In these earlier periods, we see other practitioners attempting tentative beginnings toward performing the functions of the present-day director.

The philosopher, Aristotle, tells us Thespis transformed the Greek dithyramb, a poetic choral form, into drama, as he spoke dialogue to a chorus and received a response, thus becoming the first actor-playwright. Later, Roman sources add that Thespis toured with his company of players on a wagon and was the leader of the troupe. We know the first two Greek playwrights, whose works are preserved, Aeschylus and Sophocles, choreographed the dances for their choruses.

This playwright as director tradition continued in Elizabethan England where Shakespeare is reputed to have helped stage his plays, as well as act in the company at the Globe Theatre. Yet, for the first two millennia of drama, we have no evidence of a sole individual guiding the actors.

This begins to change in 17th century France. We see in a preserved woodcut the comic playwright, Moliere, offering advice to his company in his play, *Impromptu at Versailles*. In the dialogue of this play, set in a rehearsal, we hear him giving his actor's stage business and "correct" line readings. He advises one player, "You must assume a sedate air, a natural tone of voice, and make the fewest gestures possible. "At the end of the rehearsal, in which he has explained in detail the behavior of each character to his actors, he concludes, "I tell you all your characters, that you may imprint them strongly in your minds. Let us begin to repeat and see how it will do." From our vantage point, Moliere would seem to have been a model *instructional director*.

For the next several centuries the star actor-manager ruled the commercial theatre. It would be his tradition to inhabit the down center stage position for much of the play, keeping the supporting actors well isolated from him on either side of the stage. It was a breach of actor etiquette if another player came any closer than six feet toward the star. The typical actor-manager would cross up center stage to achieve greater focus, the other actors then counter downstage right and left turn, and in fullback focus on the star.

Henry Irving, the famed British Victorian actor-manager, was famous for his lighting effects. In scenes where he stood with large groups around him, he chose to have only one weak motivational light on the crowd, for example, a lantern or candle. They would be in near darkness while a powerful limelight was focused on Sir Henry's face.

All this was about to change in the mid-1860s in a small German province where Georg II, Duke of Saxe-Meiningen, ruled over the area's political needs, as well as its subsidized court theatre. Trained in art and music, his interests gravitated more toward his theatre than local governance.

From the outset, he was different from actor-managers like Irving. Rather than extras being in the dark, he initiated crowd scenes in full light. He meticulously rehearsed each extra to find individual characteristics, rather than being a part of the usual indistinguishable mob, mechanically reacting on cue. Here, at last, was the emergence of the first total director, someone concerned with the entire excellence of a production.

The Duke's greatest talent was that of a visual artist. He not only designed the theatre sets, but also made a series of sketches of the play's actions that could be integrated into the blocking. We would describe this procedure today as the storyboarding dramatic composition of a plays key moments. For the first time, it was someone's job to clarify the story,

Saxe Meinger's particular use of stage triangles and characters occupying different levels on the stage was innovative, as was his use of more realistic sound effects and his insistence on the historical accuracy of stage props. The talented Duke designed sets, costumes, and the properties and interpreted the story through his sketches. The Duke chose not to work directly with the actors.

Ludwig Chroneg, a comic actor in the company, was appointed by Duke Georg to conduct the daily rehearsals. Working from the Duke's sketches, he prepared detailed blocking in which he dictated to the actors their precise positions and stage business for every moment of the production. He would, with Prussian efficiency, summon the actors to a rehearsal and at its conclusion dismiss them with the ringing of a large handbell. You might allow yourself a chuckle as you envision Chroneg's drill sergeant tactics, conditioning his actors to respond mechanically on cue, not unlike Pavlov's dog salivating when he heard his dinner bell rung. It was not until the latter decades of the 19th century that a new kind of organic blocking emerged.

Despite some misguided efforts of the persistent Chroneg, the importance of the Meiningen Company should not be underestimated. They brought about a revolutionary change in theatre production. Those who followed continued a trend away from declamation toward greater realism. With the rejection of wing-and-drop painted scenery, replaced by three-dimensional pieces, a more life-like stage environment was created. It was inevitable that actors would move away from declamatory acting. They were no longer acting in front of artificial backdrops but rather within a three-dimensional physical environment, the *box set*.

By the end of the 19th century, the French director Andre Antoine, at his *Theatre Libre* in Paris, had established an imaginary, opaque *fourth wall* downstage. Now the actors envisioned a solid separation from their audience. Often real objects and furniture were placed along the downstage curtain line. This allowed Antoine and Stanislavsky, who followed at his Moscow Art Theatre, to develop a more complex realistic acting style. These directors began to realize the vast potential and importance of theatrical space. They discovered that in this space, when augmented with the appropriate objects and furniture to create a *specific* environment, the actors and director were in possession of a golden key. It would open up an opportunity for motivated movement choices and physical actions by the actors that brought a new reality to their work. I am referring to what we now commonly refer to as the floor or ground plan.

Its careful creation continues to be essential in the preplanning of any production. Except in rare cases, it must be developed by the director in collaboration with the scenic designer and agreed upon anywhere from months to a minimum of several weeks before actual rehearsals begin. This permits construction drawings to be drafted and building begins in the scene shop.

There is an adage in the theatre, widely acknowledged by veteran directors, which states, "The skillfully constructed ground plan blocks the play." This suggests that the proper placement of objects and furniture in the play's physical space will propel actors to strong action choices appropriate for the text.

Would we then say the director is unnecessary in the blocking process? Certainly not. It does, however, suggest that blocking may be the dual function of the actors and directors working together. I will discuss this in-depth later as we progress.

Before we look at some of the major elements of a well-crafted ground plan, let us consider a poorly constructed one. Think of a realistic living room interior on a flat floor consisting of only a large comfortable chair downstage right and on the same plane, left center, a sofa. This arrangement, which you can still see in production shots in theatre periodicals of an earlier era, has long been a cliché. Its limitations are clear.

First, it has a stilted two-dimensional appearance. Because the furniture pieces are on the same plane, the actors will cross from one to the other in a direct straight line, which in itself is artificial. Further, while empty space can be dramatically effective, this ground plan has heavily underutilized its storytelling potential, not to mention its limited possibility for the actors to create physical variety. Such visual monotony can disturb any audience.

It is a directorial necessity to create a ground plan with elements that ensure the possibility to tell the play's story in visual terms. First, a superior ground plan requires entrances and exits that serve the action of the play.

Usually playwrights are aware of the actor's needs in interior sets, but occasionally their stage directions may result in trapping them in a *cul-de-sac*, which is only one entrance or exit in or out of a room. This should never happen. You don't want to see your actors bunched on one side of the stage, creating repetitive and monotonous movement patterns with frequent traffic jams. A balanced flow of movement is best achieved when there is at least one door or opening on two, or preferably, all three walls.

Levels, opportunities for contrasts in space, is also an essential element to provide actors a variety of spaces at different heights to interact with one another. Levels can effectively tell the play's story by emphasizing which characters are stronger and which weaker in a scene. They develop character relationships intangible space making it clear who is winning and who is losing, in a particular beat.

It is easy to forget that a full-length play needs to be comprised of literally hundreds of changing pictures. We are more aware of this in a film where constant cutting from one visual image to the next is more obvious. Creating visual variety in space is essential in theatre as well as film.

Take a moment to envision the range of vertical storytelling possibilities on a set where characters might lie or sit on the floor. Or perhaps occupy a single step of a shrunken living room or sit or stand on stairs of a staircase, play a brief duo scene on a landing, stand at the top of the stairs, or cross on a balcony level to speak to characters on the floor level below.

Where there are several rooms included in the ground plan, arrange them on levels at different heights. You need to create independent clusters of furniture or architectural elements that will offer your actors a variety of different spaces appropriate for diverse actions. Consider stage areas that attract small groups, like a bar, or a fireplace. Fill your ground plan with spaces that may be referred to as *conversation areas,* where smaller scenes can be played. The number of spaces needed depends on cast size. A medium- to large-sized cast will require more individual playing areas to avoid congestion and repetition.

I would suggest that even in smaller cast plays, you should plan on four or more of these *conversation areas.* Think of them as cozy spaces that can accommodate two or three characters with minimal furniture, perhaps two chairs and a side table. In a scene of two friends in conversation, both characters could be seated next to each other at a table. If the two characters conflict, both might be standing on either side or end of the table. Barriers of furniture that separate characters from one another helps the audience to understand a conflict that exists between them.

With the beginning of a new *beat,* you might choose to play the next ongoing actions in a different conversation area, taking the audience's focus, for example, from stage right to stage left or from upstage to downstage. In this staging, the audience's attention is continuously engaged; a certain subliminal energy is created for the audience and the monotony of sustained visual composition is avoided.

The stage director, much like the film director, is blocking the play in full stage long shots, medium shots, and close-ups to clarify its story and its momentum. Gifted playwrights instinctively create this kind of visual variety.

Think of Shakespeare who was employing film techniques centuries before the camera. The permanent architecture of his Elizabethan stage involved more conversation areas than many modern directors create in their ground plans.

For example, a clown, might sit on the edge of the apron joking with the groundlings in the audience. Major action scenes could be played on the forestage immediately behind him. Other characters might plot conspiracies or observe others from around the stage pillars that support the balcony. Upstage of them is a smaller recessed inner stage with a curtain that opens to reveal different locales, often used in domestic scenes. The stairs to the balcony provide a space for lovers to cuddle, or perhaps there might be swashbuckling swordplay up and down them. The shallow upper balcony stage, like the inner below stage, has a curtain in front of it where characters might spy on the action of a scene taking place below. This balcony curtain can open as well to reveal another interior scene. It might be Juliet's bedroom as she comes out of it onto the balcony and spies a figure on the ground below. Romeo begins to climb the pillar that now becomes a wall to reach her. He must take cover behind it as the nurse flings open one of the rose windows located on the right and left of the theatre's facade, another conversation area, as she calls Juliet to come to bed.

Shakespeare's stage, which provides nonstop action with its continuous flow of movement, moment after moment without blackouts, still instructs and inspires 21st-century directors. While Elizabethan architecture designs, may not be used in its original form it is adopted in subtle ways in a great number of contemporary Shakespearean productions.

Plan for unimpeded pathways through all your stage areas. Your production will require some space that may be needed for climatic moments of the play. Often directors choose to put such scenes downstage. These moments will be powerful close-ups.

Your objective is to create a balance between an obstacle course and open spaces. Work to create clear pathways while finding furniture as well as objects that create physical obstacles which can visually suggest a character's intentions, that have been challenged or stalled. This is an important element in communicating the play's story. So, should you believe the adage, "An outstanding ground plan blocks the play?" Of course, it does not; it is human directorial and actor ingenuity that blocks the play. Nonetheless, the thoughtful choices of furniture placement, that suggest either character connection or conflict, with multiple conversation areas that allow the actor movements to flow filmically in a variety of longs, mediums, and close-ups, will significantly enhance your probability for a well-staged play.

When you arrive at your first blocking rehearsal, you will have clearly defined your *conversation areas*. It will be helpful to tape your ground plan on the floor of your rehearsal space. It will save time later if you walk your entire cast through each of the defined spaces on the set so they may, from the beginning, understand the overall position of furniture and conversational areas. Early mastery of the ground plan will eliminate your actor's later confusions. You might further consider numbering each of the conversation areas to promote easy communication with your cast. With these numbers you can tell your actors, "Cross to area six," and so on.

Now, we are prepared to explore the coaching director's new approach to blocking. Breakaway from the fading traditions of instructional directors. As coaching directors, we will embrace a system of collaborative blocking, many directors have been working with it for decades, but none with more insight and wit than the legendary director Peter Brook, as he explains in his important book *The Empty Space.*

He tells us he was invited in his early twenties to direct *Love's Labour's Lost* at the Stratford-on-Avon Shakespeare Festival. Brooks shares with his readers, his anxieties, and how he would gain greater acceptance from the producers if he arrived with carefully planned blocking. He therefore scrupulously pre-blocked on paper, the first court scene involving 40 actors. He created as well several cardboard cutouts and various charts. After several trial and error ventures, he was certain he had a definitive blocking plan. Brook marched with alacrity into the rehearsal hall for his first staging session. His confidence bolstered by his elaborate paste-ups and detailed promptbook. Then he describes, as he enters the rehearsal hall how his misplaced security evaporated:

"As the actors began to move, I knew it was no good. These were not remotely like my cardboard figures, these large human beings thrusting themselves forward, some too fast with lively steps I had not foreseen.... We had only done the first stage of the movement, letter 'A' on my chart, but already no one was rightly placed and movement 'B' could not follow."

Brook relates his sense of panic. He knew he was well-prepared, but how was he to deal with his actors? He considered repeating his directions until they could replicate his written blocking notes. He was poised to do so, but suddenly had a revelation:

"My pattern was much less interesting than this new pattern that was unfolding in front of me, rich in energy, full of personal variation, shaped by individual enthusiasm and laziness, promising such different rhythms, opening up so many unexpected possibilities."

Brook's insight at that moment perhaps changed his life, as it certainly contributed to his brilliant career ahead.

"I stopped and walked away from my book, in amongst the actors and I have never looked at a written plan since. I recognized once and for all the presumption and folly of thinking that an inanimate model can stand for a man."

I spoke earlier of Stanislavski evolving more slowly in his career, but arriving at the same conclusion. Indeed, you might interview any number of contemporary directors, including your author, who have had similar experiences to those of Peter Brook. Although most of us, I suspect, didn't make the discovery so quickly or under such daunting circumstances. Today we are seeing, a new more collaborative spirit as directors and actors come together to accomplish the blocking process. The degree to which this collaboration occurs varies among directors. The system I will advocate here, is currently in use by several professional directors: It is the five-step mini-unit, I introduced briefly in Chapter 1. I suggested its values as an organizational method of efficiency, as well as a time-saving device that can speed up the learning curve for the actors in their work.

Now we need to look at it in detail as a vital rehearsal process that breaks out of long-held traditions and charts a new course for coaching directors and their actors. You may recall this procedure deals with dividing your play into approximately five-page units in which you will explore the blocking process in tandem with *given circumstances, improvs,* and *psychological actions.* By combining these rehearsal essentials in your initial blocking of the text, you are bringing together a process that I believe should never be separated, but almost always is in the traditional rehearsal schedule. With this approach, you have all the elements needed for your actors to grasp *physical* and *psychological actions* simultaneously with an awareness that would ordinarily only be gained much later in conventional rehearsals.

The five components of rehearsing the mini-unit are:

1. *Discuss it*
2. *Improv it*
3. *Action it*
4. *Stage it*
5. *Run it, evaluate it*

Let us look at each of these elements and how they interact.

I. Discuss It

This is a distilled version of traditional table work. I mentioned this process in the last chapter on exploratory rehearsals. My intent there was to introduce a number of exercises that involve your actors in specific exercises that give them significant needed character information relatively quickly, rather than the extended discussions of table work which while helpful, can be extremely time-consuming.

There is a story of the 1920s Broadway director Arthur Hopkins who kept his actors seated at a table discussing his productions almost until they opened. When he finally allowed them onstage, they were so pent-up with frustrated energy that they frantically blocked the play in several days and were ready for an audience.

Perhaps it worked, but it certainly seems like a curious allotment of precious rehearsal time. I prefer to digest the play with my cast as we move through five-page mini-units.

Your discussion should begin following a reading the mini-unit. Your job, as always, is to ask the right questions: Where are you? When is it? What do you need from your partners in the scene? Why are you doing the actions you are currently engaged in? The actions are the events in the scene. What happens and what changes in the life of the characters? Ask them to identify the central event of the unit. If any cast member is mistaking or overlooking it, you need to guide them. Work to be sure all of the playwright's exposition is clear. Investigate possible subtext.

This is an ideal time as well for each actor to get in touch with their *physical condition* in the mini scene. They are cool, they are warm, they are fighting drowsiness, their pulse is beating fast. Ask them to choose one simple sensory choice that will enable them to identify with the atmosphere of the scene. The actors' experience of *physical condition*, can create audience empathy. Finally, if it is relevant in a unit, you may wish to comment briefly on social, historical, or cultural issues you have gathered in your research of the play that might kindle the actor's imagination.

II. Improv It

The second element to explore in the mini-unit is improvisation. In each of these early units, you should develop a single improv to explore *given circumstances* that need further clarification.

For instance, in the first mini-unit of Chekhov's play *The Seagull*, Konstantin Treplev, a struggling young writer, the son of a celebrated veteran actress, Irina Arkadina, feels thwarted by her controlling behavior and revolts against what he considers to be her old-fashioned acting style. Here it would be helpful to improv the presentation of Treplev's new form of theatre and his mother's reaction to it. By doing so the actors can more completely explore the mother-son relationship.

These first two components of the mini-unit, discussion, and improv' can challenge your actors. They should realize general statements and vague responses to a text are not acceptable. The character's circumstances must be carefully deduced and broken open.

After your actors have developed an improv in perhaps half-a-dozen mini-units, they may have gained the essential background information they need. You might choose to drop this procedure from the mini-unit process, as it continues, leaving more time to explore the other four. You may however, need to return to improvs in later rehearsals when a scene is going stale. Improv can help the actors get back into the moment.

Now, in all likelihood, if your actors are secure with these first two steps, they may be feeling like racehorses, yearning to leave the starting gate and plant their feet on the turf. They are thinking, "Let's get on stage and start blocking." I would say, "Whoa, not so fast." Why? Because to start blocking now would be reverse logic. It is placing the play's cart before that anxious horse. The blocking should not move forward before the actors can empower it. That power is *psychological actions*. It is the actor's choices of strong verbs that create forward momentum. When the actors know what they want, from whom and why, then blocking can be effectively achieved.

Yes, a skillfully designed ground plan will help you start the blocking engine. It can motivate a flow of movement that will take your actors from point A to point B. But this is only the mechanics of the craft. If a character's truthful needs are to be discovered in a scene, the actor's *psychological actions* must be known and precede every movement in the play. So, is it not clear how futile it is for a director to block an entire play, before the start of rehearsals and likely before casting has begun? How can they expect to have insight into the possible hundreds of choices that their actors will make? Yet this has been the assumption. How accurate or complete can the director's insights be before they hear their actors' voices and sees them in action before them? If only all directors could have Peter Brook's insight.

Brook mentally threw his promptbook and paper cutouts into the air, let them float to the ground, and began his first rehearsal again. We have heard Stanislavski, early, in a long career, tell an actor on what line to exhale cigarette smoke. By the end of Stanislavski's career, when asked a question by a young actor about a choice they might make, he replies, "I don't know, what you do think?" Such behavior by masters should give even the most fervent instructional director pause.

Please do not interpret that I am advocating that your work on blocking begins in rehearsals. Throughout these pages I have suggested the need for careful study of your play, that comes from a close, critical examination of the text. I believe crucial tentative blocking choices need to be considered by the director, before the beginning of rehearsals. I will discuss this in our next step as we enter into our collaborative actor/director blocking process.

III: Action It

I have now, hopefully, made the case that we must reverse the old order of blocking the play. All that is essential in this phase of the work is to identify what the characters need from each other and how they will fulfill their needs. Ask your actors before beginning their scene work to consider their verb choices in the mini-unit.

Inquire if there might be a clue in the text as to what they want from their partner. Does the verb itself evoke a mental picture of how they will achieve their goal? Remind them that they should think in the first person and verbalize: I want, I need, or I must, depending on the intensity of their desire. Next, having verbalized their intention, they should justify their goals with the word "because."

Note that I am asking you to continue to function in a Socratic mode. You are asking questions and expecting your actors to respond. Urge them to make specific and positive choices with strong verbs. Be prepared that they may be tentative at the outset of this work. Let your actors know that their initial responses may change as rehearsals continue. Together you are building a process that will produce highly creative results. Don't expect all the power verbs that create the strongest actor choices to emerge at the beginning. This work needs to ripen.

For some of your actors, this may be the first time they have dealt with *psychological actions*. Without judgment, offer them a verb if they are hesitant or stalled. Be diplomatic with statements like, "You might consider the verb _____." Ask if their choice offers the possibility for an action. If you sense they are close to an appropriate verb choice but not yet specific enough, ask them to give synonyms. The stronger, more appropriate verb may emerge. Counsel them in their preparation to consult the dictionary and/or a thesaurus for inspiration.

Before this first blocking, you will have done your homework and made several verb choices for each *psychological action* you consider possible for the characters. This is another benefit of working with these shorter units. It will require relatively brief preparation time to either review the verb choices you have previously chosen or choose them before your blocking rehearsal.

A director needs to have humility when an actor suggests an action verb superior to their own. The *action it* mini-unit work needs to deal with two further elements I identified in the 10 essentials chapter: *obstacles* and *beats*. An actor usually quickly identifies the obstacle. The one question the director asks is: What is getting in the way of what you want from the other character? The answer is usually instantaneous because it is often obvious. If it appears to be ambiguous or the actor is unable to respond to the question, do not move on until there is clarity.

Discovering *beats* is a continuous process for you and your actors. In the traditional rehearsal schedule, this work often does not occur until later. Here, however, I encourage you to guide your actors early in the mini-blocking units, as they transition from one *psychological action* to the next, this is the *beat change*. This will give them a longer period to experiment and make subtle changes in their interpretation as they discover more nuances in the script.

As your cast moves through *psychological actions*, they must choose exactly where in the script to move from one beat to next. Your actors will pause, breathe, and make a discovery of a new intention and these choices may also change during rehearsals.

These physical and mental transitions will lead your actors to their next *psychological action*. If the end of the last *beat* was inconclusive, there was no clear victory or defeat; the character will need to continue the pursuit of their same need with the same verb, but a new tactic. If they have won or lost the *beat*, they will shift to a new line of thought and a different verb. A first decision on a *beat change* should not be cast in granite. This process should come early in rehearsals and should be experimented with until the play closes. When careful attention is given to shaping *beats*, the actor creates a structure and rhythm that builds interest through a variety in pace and duration of pauses that increases the clarity of the play's story.

IV: Stage It

Your actors, armed with their insight from the previous three steps, "*discuss it*," "*improv it*," and "*action it*," are ready to get on their feet and experience the play in movement. We need to look at what collaborative blocking entails. Instructional blocking was entirely director-centered. Do we switch now to a system that is all actor-initiated? I think not. The word *collaborative* suggests continuous interaction. It may be helpful if I first separate the actors' and director's roles for clarity. Here are some thoughts about the director's pre-production planning of blocking.

How much and to what kind of blocking preparation prior to rehearsals should the coaching director be committed. This depends on your temperament and comfort zone for spontaneity, though I recommend minimal to moderate. The minimal I have in mind is identifying in your director's script in what stage area you want each scene played and the movement changes from one *conversation area* to another. This is necessary because the director should be responsible for the visual flow of the movement of an entire production.

In the earlier discussion of the traditional Shakespearean stage, I spoke of a continuing film-like movement of shots—long, medium, and close-ups. The director should always have this kind of variety in mind. Allowing your actors to make their choice of area location may not lead to chaos, but it will likely restrict the pictorial flow and variety the play requires. Actors with freedom of choice may be inclined, not unlike the actor-managers of old, to play an overabundance of scenes in center stage or its immediate suburbs.

Your preparation needs will guide you to how much pre-blocking you do. Working with short, five-minute units makes it far easier for you to prepare the next set of blocking choices between rehearsals. This is more practical than pre-blocking choices long in advance, as the retention of your choices will be far greater.

When you ask your actors to join you in the blocking of the production, you are building company morale. Actors will take greater pride in the work when they have a strong voice in this creative input. However, asking actors cold on their feet to create blocking choices, places them in a somewhat vulnerable position. Some of your actors might not have worked this way before. They may freeze under this pressure and be unable to respond. You should be ready to offer at least two examples of blocking directions if they falter. Whether you carry this information in your head or need to consult your working script is your decision. You will know how you best function.

The most effective question you can ask your actors in these collaborative blocking sessions is, "What does your *psychological action* suggest you should *do* at this moment?" Does your verb suggest physical actions for your character? The stronger the choices the actors have made about the character's needs in the *action it* section, the easier it will be for them to initiate effective movement in the *stage its* rehearsals. All initial blocking should be recorded in their scripts.

Not only should you come to the aid of your actors with your blocking choices when they are challenged, but there will likely be some key actions you will want to stage yourself. These textual moments involve important images you would like to share with the audience. These choices are the director's responsibility. They are the visual composition storytelling that you create to clarify the plot, theme, and concept. They often involve a bold personal image. Besides, you may wish in these first blocking rehearsals to suggest some stage business or character behavior that involves handling props.

In your earliest rehearsals, you made a commitment to your actors that this would be an ensemble production. Collaborative blocking fulfills that pledge and sends the message that they have both the opportunity and responsibility of owning their characters' lives.

V: Run it, Evaluate it

You have just completed the first tentative blocking of the mini-unit. Check for any trouble spots that may need revision. If there are, discuss them and make any minor adjustments. Now, ask your actors to attempt a first nonstop reading while moving through their blocking. The actors need to get a sense of continuity and rhythm. Tell your actors you will give them comments following the run through.

Hopefully the blocking will be logical and a sense of the intended dramatic values will emerge. If stops have to be made to address problems, you will need to decide about rehearsal time, as you will have scheduled for only one run-through. If your actors seem insecure or dispirited with the results, borrow some time from the rehearsal bank to fix the problems and run the unit again.

When you offer comments, you may be making another departure from established rehearsal procedure. Directors often begin notes after actors are off book on a section. It has been my experience that they welcome specific comments as early as possible. You have the obligation to make your notes as encouraging and positive as possible.

To be critical and nitpicky at this early stage of the process is, to say the least, counterproductive. Your notes should deal with whatever elements are off to a good start. Discuss character relationships that are on the right track, and whatever else you might reinforce. Give your actors specific future goals. What should they work on for the next rehearsal? Can you tell them how to better motivate a specific character movement or explore a different physicalization? Your optimistic spirits will be appreciated, but you should suggest that you hope to see your comments realized in rehearsals ahead. Let them know when you will run the unit again and on what date it will be off-book. This information should be on their rehearsal schedule, as well.

I would suggest you run the same unit nonstop at the next rehearsal to help your actors solidify it and again approximately two days later with lines off. After that you will begin to work it in depth *beat* to *beat*.

As the director, you will always be the final judge of any given moment of staging. You will discover, however, that your actors' need for help in blocking will decrease as you allow them to follow their bliss and discover the life of their characters through motivating their movement. These sessions are among the strongest elements in establishing a bond with your actors. Morale in rehearsals rises as the actors change the pronoun from, "his or her production" to "our production."

The emphasis in this book changes slightly now. Up to this point, we have been sequentially tracking the work, in some sections, one rehearsal to the next. Now we are into the body of the process of the coaching director: exploring the text in detail and creating solutions to individual actor challenges. We have explained our coaching approach to exploratory and blocking rehearsals, we move on now to the polishing period. At this point, your actors will benefit when you introduce them to side coaching. You may be familiar with this procedure which allows them to continue speaking their dialogue while you simultaneously feed them oral directions. Your brief verbal directions to the actors in side-coaching will accomplish a number of major goals. First, you encourage actors through positive feedback. Ask them to strengthen a moment saying, "Great! You are on the right track, go further be bolder here, or you have almost got it, now pull back just a bit.!"

Then, when you need to change a mood or create a strong atmosphere, offer a powerful mental image: "It is 3 am, you're exhausted, struggling to focus on your partner through the dense mental fog you are experiencing." Next, strengthen the actor's psychological action. For example, you need to make a stronger argument. "Be a drill that bores into his skull", or change a relationship, "You know she's suspicious of you, calm him as if you were his respected family doctor."

Obviously, you need to be both precise and concise with your words. Make your comments immediately clear and brief, so the actor doesn't drop out of the scene. Side coaching should never become an irritant. It should have the quality of calm friendly advice. Certainly, you should not be shouting from the middle of the house. You need to be close to your actors. You may be on stage almost whispering to them. Used wisely at appropriate moments, side coaching is a valuable addition to the coaching director skills.

The next four chapters are geared to offer as many possible solutions to your actors' challenges as space allows. In the next chapter we will look at imagination, the nature of images, and the process by which actors develop them.

6

Imagination And Images

D irectors are often encouraged when polishing rehearsals begin and sparks start flying as actors are beginning to become invested in the world of the play and its circumstances. When this happens, it is as if their creative motors had been idling; now they suddenly shift into gear, feeling their power. Technically, it is the moment when the actors' concentration and imagination merge. You realize, nonetheless, that a considerable journey lies ahead.

Do not misunderstand; I am not disparaging all the work the cast has developed to this point. The actors' exploration through given circumstances, improvisations, and choosing *psychological actions* is an essential process that will produce this new period of truthful moments. In our six-and-a-half-week rehearsal schedule, I would anticipate this happening sometime between the second and third week of rehearsal.

Stanislavski described this experience in his groundbreaking book, *An Actor Prepares*. In his chapter on imagination, he tells actors: "We must have a solid line of inner visions … out of these moments will be formed an unbroken series of images, something like a moving picture. As long as we are acting creatively, this film will unroll and be thrown on the screen of our inner vision, making vivid the circumstance among which we are moving."

This is a highly incisive description of how imagination triggers the acting process. I have found, however, that actors are often inclined to take these words too literally. You may remind your actors that their five senses are the key to these "inner visions" and the pathway to igniting their emotions. Yes, images are often pictures and the visual sense is an important one, but do not let your actors make them exclusively visual. The other four senses are equally and sometimes more helpful.

Consider, for example, the image of the odor of a particular scent of perfume that an actor recalls from personal experience and uses in connecting with his partner in a love scene. Or, the sound of chalk squeaking on a blackboard that viscerally puts him on edge with irritation in a scene where they know another character is lying to him. Or again, the actor may discover how a tiny taste of vinegar or honey on his tongue will instantly change his relationship with the other character. Recalling an icy cold shower could give them the emotional stimulus the needs in a scene where they encounter a robber brandishing a gun inches from their face.

The "inner visions" Stanislavski speaks of may certainly be visual. They have their special place. However, *any* stimulus that ignites the actor's imagination can be powerful. It is when this concentration is lost and there is nothing behind the actor's eyes or any physical stimulus in their body that the deadly empty sign flashes on.

Therefore, I urge you to work with your actors on sensory images, sight yes, but putting an equal emphasis on smell, sound, taste, and touch, as well. You should be prepared, initially, to feed your actors images. Some, who have not experienced sensory work, may need to be spoon-fed. You will observe which of your actors need more image stimulus and work with them creatively. This may be done in note sessions, but it is more effective in personal coaching. Some directors like to momentarily stop a scene to whisper an image idea to an actor. This can be effective, though I would not recommend it be overdone. It can be rude and irritating to the other actors.

I would, suggest rather offering images at the end of scenes or in a private so your actors may think about them for their next rehearsal.

Be confident of your abilities to give actors vivid sensory images when needed. The most helpful advice I can offer is to think hot and cold about dramatic moments. What is it like when ice is held for minutes in your hand, or a match is burning out on your fingertips? Suggest crunchy snow, intense heat, or a painful sunburn. Images may be literal, relating to the real events of a scene, but often metaphors and similes of basic sensory experience can be more powerful and lead the actor to highly charged acting moments.

For those in your cast already working with sensory images, they will need only your encouragement to keep creating them. Do not be concerned that your input will stifle those actors who have not worked in this way before by treading on their creative work. It is a good strategy to say, "Here's an image that may work for you, play with it and create your own version of it."

Let us turn now to some specific exercises you can introduce if some of your actors are new to this process. A short image warm-up session should begin these rehearsals. It is best to introduce or review simple visual images first; the other four senses should quickly follow.

Exercise #1
Empty to Filled Nouns

The director and the actors relax, sitting preferably in a circle. Explain to the cast that you will point to an actor who should respond quickly and automatically after you speak a word that is a noun. They should repeat the word as quickly and blankly as possible without meaning or visualization. Then the actor takes a quick moment, catches their image, attitude, or association toward this person, place or thing, and repeats the word filled with their personal responses to it. If I say, "Abraham Lincoln," the actor repeats the name immediately before thinking or feeling. They then repeat it, using their sensory, individual responses to that president.

The name will come alive; it will be *personalized*. If you say, "London," to the next actor, they should first experience a blank screen. When they repeat the word, they may use visualization and perhaps other senses as well. It will be equally vivid if it is an actual personal recall of having visited that city or an imaginative image of being there. The point is once the actor freely associates with their senses the words come alive. A small moment of reality is created.

A mosaic of these moments makes a filled and dynamic performance, achieving Stanislavski's, "solid line of inner visions." As you continue with the exercise, emphasize those nouns classified as things. Common objects are quick and easy to evoke. Thus, the exercise may continue as you say, "popcorn," "cell phone," "light bulb," "tulip," "ceiling fan," "VCR," "doormat," etc. This is, the quickest and most effective way to initiate image-making. If this is either a new concept for the actor or a previously learned but neglected one, mastery can be acquired in a short period of time.

Exercise #2

The Image Trunk

Continue the image work with this enjoyable exercise. It is similar to *Empty to Filled Nouns* but has the added advantage of relying more strongly on the actor's recollections and memories. A cast member stands ready as you offer these *given circumstances*: you are alone in the attic of your childhood home; you spot an old family trunk. Curiosity compels you to open it. As the director announces an individual item in the trunk, the actor will lift the imaginary object out, hold it in their hands, examine it, and create imaginary or real sensorial associations with the object. Perhaps they demonstrate the object's function. When they complete their examination, they place it back in the trunk. As the next object is announced, another actor lifts it out, creating their sensory impressions.

The exercise is most effective when you suggest items that might commonly be associated with the actor's childhood or adolescence. A typical list could include: a tennis racquet, Raggedy Ann doll, waffle iron, high school yearbook, catcher's mitt, birthday card, Christmas ornament, etc. Some of these items may indeed evoke emotional memories for the actor, which creates the strongest of sensory images. You will note how each object affects your actors; when you see a strong response, you may allow them more time to explore it.

This exercise takes the actors a step forward from the *Empty to Filled Nouns* word game as they are now dealing with more than just imagined pictures. Here, as they involve all their senses, both psychological and physical responses occur. Their mind and body simultaneously remember and experiences the imaginary object they are exploring.

This exercise replicates what you are guiding your actors to do with the text. These two group exercises are enjoyable to work on and they introduce or review the key aspects of acting with imagination in a minimal amount of rehearsal time. If there are cast members that you sense need more work in creating sense imagery, suggest the following exercises for them to try on their own.

Exercise #3

A Year's Passage

This kind of transformation exercise was developed by the famed actor and acting coach Michael Chekhov. Have your actors first with eyes closed to create a landscape. Suggest to them they visualize a farm in winter, a house and barn surrounded by apple trees. There is heavy snow on the ground. Have them explore this scene first in their mind's eye; then, ask them to enter into the atmosphere of this scene using all of their senses. Experience the cold, touch the snow, perhaps they will put a dab on their tongue, or make a snowball. What odors do they sense in the yard? What winter sounds surround them?

Ask the actors now to open their eyes and keep exploring this scene. Have them now transform the scene to spring. Ask them to repeat the same careful process, experiencing, sense by sense, in this season. Request that they keep all their senses simultaneously alive.

Then, transform the scene to summer. They should see and smell the trees as they continue to bloom. Are there farm animals in the yard? What are the surrounding odors? Have the actors touch the apple tree, pick and taste an apple, and experience the summer heat.

Now they transform to autumn and with eyes open, using all their senses, explore the landscape until the seasonal cycle is complete. For your actors who may wish to continue this sensory exploration work, an element of fantasy is added in the next exercise.

Exercise #4
The Impossible Made Possible

The actors, now working with their eyes open from the beginning of the exercise, create the picture of an automobile junkyard. They see there an older car recognized as a model from several decades ago. They come closer to it and view the peeling paint and rust. They touch their hands over its rough surface. They hear a slight creak as they open the door and look inside, smelling an odor of mold from the upholstered car seats. The chrome on the dashboard is badly tarnished. The actors take a few steps back and observe its outside appearance, much as if they were an artist about to paint it. Ask the actors to freeze-frame that image for a moment. They etch in their imagination as specific and detailed a reconstruction of the car, as possible.

Now, in slow motion, starting at the front grill, ask them to begin to transform the old car into a sleek new model of their dreams, perhaps a Mercedes, or for practicality, they may prefer a Prius. The actor follows Stanislavski's advice: "Find an unbroken series of images ...." Frame-by-frame, they allow the old car to meld into a new reality. Let them savor the process of the change of line, form, texture, and color. Finish the exercise as they open the silent car door, slide into its luxurious leather seats, turn the key in the ignition, and speed out of the junkyard onto the freeway.

Continued practice with these kinds of sensory exercises will build the actors' concentration and confidence in their imagination and its application to their textual image work.

As we return now to our script, we will explore four areas in which the actors put to work their imagination and imagery process on the play. They are: *The Given Circumstances*, *The actor's physical condition*, *substitution images*, and *personal world Fantasy Images*.

Exercise #5
Turning Given Circumstances into Images

The script's *given circumstances* are an essential source of the actors' imagery. The probing of who, what, where, when, why—the Five Elementary W's are crucial to the actor's success in bringing the script vividly alive for an audience. How do the actors distill this background information? They first take from the script the important incidents from the characters' past life and imagine them fully.

Suggest to your actors that they close their eyes, let their senses go to work, and allow their inner visions to flow, especially those things that the character knows well or is passionate about. These need to be envisioned again and again. They should explore these images of their character's life until they have bonded with them.

A strong example of the world of the play's given circumstance images could be scene two of Tennessee William's poignant, *The Glass Menagerie*. Laura has been confronted by her Mother, Amanda for lying about attending business school when she was actually absent, fantasizing in her imagination while at a local park. Amanda relentlessly questions her daughter about her whereabouts. Laura then tells her mother about the glasshouse in the zoo, and the penguins there. When she becomes more distressed over her mother's questioning, she cries out to her, "You look like the picture of Jesus' Mother in the museum." It is a vivid scene in which the actress Laura must do her image homework. She needs ideally to visit a zoo, certainly to observe penguins, pick a specific painting of the Madonna and work and rework these images in her imagination.

She should then in rehearsal and performances project them out a few feet toward Amanda in the scene and if the director wants Laura to turn away from her mother and be more open at some point in the speech, she needs to be able to project her images out, making the back of the theatre her fourth wall.

Exercise #6
The Actor's Physical Condition

What I am referring to here is the atmospheric element(s) of the scene. I would define it as the character's sensory experience at this precise moment. It is relatively easy for the actor to create because it usually deals with the outward elements of weather. It is hot, it is cold, you are sunburnt, your lips are chapped. Or, it may be an outward manifestation of an inner emotional state. Your palms are sweating, there is a nervous tic in your left eye, and you are slightly hyperventilating.

The *physical condition* of the characters helps create the mood of a scene and may offer psychological clues about the characters' behavior. It allows the actors to be more accessible and vulnerable to an audience. Directors can greatly increase the power of a scene by feeding actors sensory images of a *physical condition* in preparation for an entrance.

Let me illustrate with an example of an earlier moment in the same scene in *The Glass Menagerie*, in which you would suggest weather and *given circumstance* as *physical condition* images for your actors. The scene begins with Laura home alone in one of her favorite pastimes, playing an old phonograph record. She hears her mother coming up the steps. She hurriedly shuts off the music and moves as rapidly as she can to the typewriter to pretend to practice her imagined classwork. The *given circumstance* of the scene for her Mother Amanda is that she has just been to the business school to check up on Laura's progress, and was told she had dropped out some time ago.

You could give your actress Amanda the following additional circumstances and sensory images. Hearing the distressing news of Laura's deceit, she has walked home almost in a stupor. It is an unseasonably cold day, 20 degrees below normal and she is wearing her old thin coat, bought years ago in Mississippi, more suitable for the warmer weather there. Here, in St. Louis, she is chilled to the bone. She enters the apartment and sees Laura at her assumed typing practice. Amanda rails out at her, "deception, deception, deception." Her frigid sensory experience will work as a strong physical condition for the emotional scene as she shivers in cold rage at her daughter.

Physical condition images heighten the reality, complement the play's *given circumstances,* and build the mood of a scene. Be alert, directors, to what a difference weather can make!

Exercise #7
Substitution Images

This technique refers to your actors searching for an experience in their life parallel, or at least closely similar to the event in the play, and merging personal remembrance into images that are appropriate to evoke the character's emotion.

First, you need to be sensitive that your actor's personal experiences are their private life. They have no obligation to reveal them to the director. To do so may be a violation of their privacy and it can be artistically invalid as well.

All you need to do is ask the question, "What is your personal experience is closest to your character's emotion in this scene? You don't need to reveal it to me, just take a moment to think about it and get in touch with it using all of your senses."

Give your actor some time; move on to ask a question, or the same one of another actor. Return to your first actor and ask if they have a *substitution image*? If they nod yes, say, "don't tell me, let's just begin to work." If they say, "No, not yet," you might say to them, "Think about it tonight," and then you might steal a line from the famous British director Sir Tyrone Guthrie, who would say to his actors, "Astonish us in the morning." Part of your job is to encourage actor preparation away from rehearsals.

I have spoken of the importance of the director assuming a Socratic method to keep asking the Five Elementary W questions. Socrates, the great ancient Greek philosopher, was called the Gadfly because, like a stable fly, he stung or annoyed his fellow citizens of Athens to make them think. The dictionary is rather hard on that old insect. Gadfly is now a synonym for a person "who persistently annoys or provokes others with criticism, ideas, demands, or requests." If we insert the word "gentle" before "criticism" in the above definition, it may be an excellent description for the coaching director.

Let us return to *The Glass Menagerie* to encounter the actress playing Laura searching for a *substitution image* in the gentleman caller scene. The doorbell rings and Laura limps to the door. She has a physical impediment and wore a leg brace in high school; she has magnified what may be a slight disability into an acute inferiority complex that makes her excessively shy and reclusive.

She opens the door to see her brother, Tom, who has brought his friend, Jim, for a dinner date with Laura. Jim and Laura were acquaintances in high school, but he does not now immediately recognize her. Laura, on the other hand, had a serious crush on him and is still attracted, but her instinct is to retreat from him. This is the moment in which the actress requires a *substitution image*.

Our actress went home, did her actor homework, and is prepared to astonish us this morning. She does not reveal her *substitution* to the director or other actors. She begins the scene. She had remembered as a sophomore in high school that she had a bad case of acne on the left side of her face and would turn her right profile towards others at every opportunity. She makes use of this personal memory in the scene. As she opens the door and sees Jim, she turns her body to the left facing him in right profile, which makes the moment uncomfortable. Her character appears awkward and somewhat confused. The power of her emotional memory gives Laura a strong impetus to play the rest of the short beat. The director tells her it was an authentic moment and compliments her by saying it was the best she has played it.

Then, the Gadfly director responds with more questions: "How serious is Laura's limp and how will you develop it? Would you work more on physicalizing that for tomorrow?" She says yes, then asks, "May I talk to you after rehearsal?" They sit and relax in the green room after the others have gone. "I want to share my *substitution* with you," she says. "Go ahead, certainly." (Being a wise director, he knows sharing personal images should always be the actor's choice.)

She confides about her painful acne experience and how it made her turn away from people. She tells the director this experience made her feel detached from classmates. The director tells her it is a great analogous choice for Laura. She says she wonders if it will work because she agrees with his implication that the scene is not about acne, but rather the limp. "One step at a time," the director tells her. "Powerful acting is about finding multiple choices in a scene. You should keep the *substitution* of the acne, but you might add to your backstory that Laura had an extremely mild case of polio as a child but has essentially recovered. Her conditioning limp seems somehow a comfort to her. Our actress thinks it is an excellent idea.

"Laura's problems now, she says" are essentially psychological. "Yes" responds the director, but keep working physically, our work is all trial and keep exploring our work is all trial and error." They say goodnight and go their separate ways. This give and take between actor and director is crucial to the rehearsal process.

Actors in my rehearsals frequently asked me about this process of *Substitution*, which is often referred to as *emotional memory*. Is it strictly a technique in which the actor, using personal experiences in rehearsals, continues to use them in performance? My answer is an ambiguous it all depends. I think most fine actors would say their imagination begins to work when they bring to life a vivid memory of a personal feeling toward a person, place, or object and create it through a physical sensory moment. This memory clings to that particular feeling until it stops being an aspect of their private life and becomes part of their relationship with another character. In other words, hopefully, the actor's emotional life transforms into the *given circumstances*. This may not happen. Until it does, the actor keeps evoking their real memory, keeping all the circumstances fresh. However, after multiple rehearsals they should require only a brief trigger to unlock the emotions from the sense memory event. Either way is valid as long as the actor keeps their imagery powerful.

Exercise #8
Personal World Fantasy Images

The work I have just discussed in substitution images had its origin in Stanislavski's emotional memory work at the Moscow Art Theatre and came to fruition in America in the 1930s with the work of actor coach Lee Strasberg at the Group Theatre. This highly talented ensemble of actors produced many future acting teachers and directors who influenced generations of American method actors.

"Method" denotes the teachings of Stanislavski adapted to an American sensibility. These practitioners included Harold Clurman, Stella Adler, Robert Lewis, and Sanford Meisner among many others. All were gifted and volatile. They frequently argued about acting theories among themselves to the extent of disparaging one another publicly and at times declaring a colleague fraudulent for promoting a particular principle or exercise, with which they disagreed.

Such was the case of acting coach Meisner with his fantasy technique, which he considered more viable than Strasberg's reliance on the actor's emotional substitutions. His work makes use of fantasy, a thing that never happened. Meisner called his technique appropriately, "daydreaming." He wanted his actors to create their fantasy images, to believe in them, and play them as truth. He insisted that as the actor daydreams, a transformation takes over their inner life so that they are not who they were five minutes ago because fantasy, so strongly affects the actor.

Meisner reminded us that long-ago Freud suggested that our daydreams are based on sex and ambition. He told his actors they might dream that they are accepting their academy award for best actor. Or, that they are a super-hero with the goal to save the world.

Turn back to *The Glass Menagerie*. Laura, an active daydreamer, lives vividly in a world of her own. In the "gentleman caller," scene, Jim, urges her to dance. She protests that she is physically unable to do so. He takes her in his arms and despite her impediment, they move rhythmically together. Our actress Laura could use a strong fantasy image here. Her director might suggest that she daydreams that Jim puts his arms around her waist and that they are dancing toward her favorite glass animal, the unicorn. She identi-fies with it because, like herself, it is different. As she explains, "it is extinct in the modern world." In her fantasy, she whispers to Jim to lift her onto the unicorns back. She then motions for him to join her. Laura commands the glass unicorn to fly out the window and take them to that perfect world where they might live happily-ever-after.

Directors who encourage personal fantasy images are likely to be rewarded with some very creative results from their actors.

A final note now on the battles of the method-acting teachers. I think it would be a mistake for your actors, as they study their theories, to take a stand and join one camp in war against another. Creative, actors have long used all these image approaches, sometimes in the same role. *Substitution* is powerful because it comes from the performer's authentic emotional life and can deeply move an audience. Personal fantasy images can open the actor's imagination and bring lighter more playful or bizarre original moments to their work.

In addition to *Substitution* and *Personal Fantasy*, there is a third major preparation approach in creating imagery you should urge your actors to explore—*The World of the Play*.

It begins, as all rehearsals should, with actors identifying the *given circumstances* of the script. They will write in their journals each verifiable fact about their character that the playwright offers. With this information, they then enter the imaginative state of inner images. They begin to transform the dry facts of their character's lives into vivid sense impressions that affect both their mind and bodies. The facts slowly will take on emotional characteristics that can lead the characters to specific creative choices.

The actors should not just visualize images involved in the action of the story, but should work intensely to touch, taste, smell, and hear all the stimuli possible that surrounds the events of the scene.

Ask your actors to involve themselves in this experience away from rehearsals. They should close their eyes and see their characters in physical actions. How do they walk across a room, make coffee, brush their teeth? Then, they should go inside the play, see the locale in detail where their story begins and work to experience their *physical condition* in the scene. This process resembles *Substitution,* but rather than the actors using themselves in the *given circumstances*, they are working on the text word by word, moment by moment to allow *it* to become the reality that pulls them into the world of the play.

I suggest you expose your actors to all three of these preparations. Creative actors often use them in combination. You need to have a variety of techniques at your disposal to address a particular problem because of your actor's differences, life experiences, and tolerance for risk.

In the course of the rehearsal sometimes images can fade or momentarily blackout and the actor has to reach for fresh imaginative stimuli in a scene. In the section ahead, I will discuss the use of images in the areas of inner monologue and imagery associated with objects or props. Imagery may sometimes involve a mental process that is more verbal than sensory. I would define an image as *any* valid stimulus actors use to sustain their concentration and imagination that will ensure a continuous stream of inner activity in their performance.

What happens if this process of interior involvement either stops or has not been undertaken? Quite simply the actor goes blank because they are devoid of any inner inspiration. A discerning audience member will perceive their blank stare, as there is nothing behind their eyes. The actor has taken leave of the world of the play, becomes disconnected from their stream of stimuli, and entered a dead zone. You need to make a note of any of these moments in rehearsals so you can work with your actor to restore both their concentration and imagination.

Let us consider a precaution acting partners should take to keep their connection vital in a scene. In intense interaction among actors, you need to observe that they are not over-relying on visual imagery. Be sure they are not swept up in detailed pictures of persons, and places in the past rather than being in the present moment with each other.

This problem is what might be called the glassy eye stare syndrome. Your actor may have evocative personal or daydream images that can produce strong emotions, but if they block the reality of being connected to their partners, particularly in a moment of confrontational dialogue, there will be a problem. Strong actor connection is crucial to a play's success and the actors getting lost in their character's interior dreams must not undercut it. Such imagery of past events is most effective in solo reminiscences, monologues and soliloquies. In intense partner exchanges other approaches are needed. If your actors are overusing visual imagery in a scene, this next exercise that we call *Think/Speak* can get partners connecting again.

Exercise #9
Think/Speak

Ask your actors to back up a few lines from where a problem occurred. Request them to slow down the pace considerably as they begin the text again. Partner A delivers his line. As he speaks, partner B silently thinks his subtext to A's line. B's character may agree with A's statement or be in opposition to it. Rather than continuing the dialogue, character B now verbalizes aloud the words he just thought. He then continues with his next scripted line. As he does this, character A thinks his silent subtext response. As B finishes his textual line, A verbalizes his inner monologue line followed by his next textual line. You should proceed with the dialogue very slowly until the actors are comfortable with this process.

Now begin the scene again closer to performance tempo. The actor on his partner's line must hear in his head his subtext responses to what was just spoken, but not verbalize them aloud. Continue with this procedure until your actors are listening to and responding with each other appropriately.

This inner monologue is an important tool, to the extent that it keeps the actor's concentration and imagination sustained. It can be valuable when actors drop out of the moment, as it demands keen concentration. I recommend however, it be applied in moderation. With overuse, actors may find it ponderous or pedantic. You should encourage your actors when they are working correctly and come to their aid in helping them change direction when their work is counter-productive.

Let me offer two different imagined scenarios to clarify this by creating two actresses, working in dramatically different imagery approaches. The scene is between two lovers in a tender moment that suddenly turns to accusations and then to anger. We will first look at a skilled actress; I shall call her Jane, who will use personalization correctly. She establishes a professional relationship of respect for and sharing with her partner. She works clearly within the givens of the scene, finding sensory and other images appropriate to it. However, the trigger moment, when she must feel intense anger and have an emotional outburst targeted at her boyfriend, is not working for her.

At the end of the rehearsal, the director speaks to her privately and suggests she work on a personal, memory of anger. Jane does her homework and considers several moments of intense anger from her personal life: one aimed at her little brother, the other at her mother when she was younger. She chooses her mother because she considers it more intense and closer to herself, though by no means is it parallel to the play's given circumstances.

She returns to the theatre to astonish her director in the morning. Jane again establishes strong eye contact and physical connection with her partner. She works within the *given circumstances.* Then she hits her trigger moment and has an emotional explosion. She hears her mother's voice, her threatening tone, and is momentarily transported to that traumatic moment in her past. Her rage is authentic and intense. Nonetheless, after a short pause, her memory evaporates and she is in the present moment in the script with her boyfriend. The events of the play only go deeper for her. The director is pleased with her work and Jane feels satisfied that she has achieved this challenge.

Now let us look at another actress. She is less experienced, but eager to succeed in the same role. I shall call her Joan. She wants the opening romantic moments of her scene to go well but she finds her male partner unattractive and overly intense. Joan missed the sessions in her acting class on contact and connection, but she loved it when they worked on imagination and images. She has a brainstorm. Instead of dealing with, in her opinion, her far-from-ideal acting partner, she will create a complete sensory picture of her real-life boyfriend and play the text with those images rather than connect with her present partner in the scene. Joan is instantly pleased with her work. She is delighted as she loses herself in the romantic memories. She almost stops breathing, her voice drops to a low audibility and she swallows the ends of her sentences. She sees her created lover so vividly that her eyes are partially shut. As she opens them wide in the anger moment, she seems to be in another world. She does not hear the words her partner is speaking. He is distressed knowing she is not listening or connecting with him.

Joan, on the other hand, is thrilled. She sees her boyfriend so completely and feels the emotion so intensely that she is trembling. She has to share her rapture with her director and tells you, "I've never been so completely lost in my own emotions before. It felt so wonderful." What do you tell her? Careful now, some tact is in order. You might respond along these lines, "It's fine to have that depth of emotion; a good actress needs it, but you must work with control and technique which wasn't happening. I could hardly hear or understand you because you had forgotten to breathe. It is admirable that you have the ability to imagine another human being, but you must not do it at the expense of your partner who couldn't do his work properly because you had shut him out. You both must send and receive impulses, moment by moment in the scene. Respect your partner, breathe and connect with the circumstances of the scene, and keep eye contact with him. Most importantly, you do not need all that intense outside imagery. One or two key moments of recall are all you require to make the scene work. I know you can do that, now, let's try it again."

Joan and Jane are imaginary, but, as a director coach, you will encounter their counterparts often. The Jane's are wonderful company members. The Joan's … well, that is why you are sitting in the director's chair. You will develop the tact, patience, and skill to help them use their natural, rather than their misguided talents, and help them to merge with the acting ensemble.

Exercise # 10
Furniture & Props

While working to help your actors find reality in their roles, it may feel like a full-time job, however, the coaching director needs to give attention as well as breathing life into inanimate objects. Not all relationships on stage need be human; the furniture in your production can enhance your actor's characterizations. By this time in your rehearsal process, you and your scene designer have likely finalized the furniture choices of your set. If it's not yet available, take a few minutes in rehearsal to describe or better yet show the cast photos of these pieces. Actors will most likely continue to rehearse with mock-ups, often-basic wooden benches, and metal folding chairs, well through the technical rehearsals. They should begin much earlier to visualize the sensory properties of the actual furniture and their emotional and psychological relationship to it. By having specific attitudes toward these objects, the actor changes these mock-up pieces into their possessions, that offer clues to their character.

Ask your actors, are these furnishings new or shabby? Are they luxury items or did they come from the local thrift store? Are they tasteful or gaudy? Do the fabrics clash or complement their character's personality? When your cast starts making choices about the objects in their environment, they deepen their characterizations. The actor's relationship with familiar furniture helps tell their story.

Urge your actors to have warm or cold, favorite, or hostile relationships with their possessions. How does the banker, who sinks with aching joints deep into the cushions of his expensive leather chair, respond? Or the family son who bangs on the near-obsolete T.V. set in such a manner to tell us he loathes this long out of date model? An audience may empathize with the older character who carefully eases himself into a rickety old rocker, which he has endowed with a broken spring that he carefully maneuvers himself away from to avoid pain and experience pleasure. Resourceful actors may lead the audience's imagination into any socio-economic, cultural, or psychological period a script requires, through their relationship to their surroundings.

Similarly, stage props are among the best friends that directors and actors have in their respective crafts. As a resourceful director, you should carefully study the prop list of your script and begin to think of specific ways the character can use these objects. Then, imagine other objects that they might engage with creativity in the play. In some plays, directors try to find a key prop for every major character that might give clues to their personality or perhaps even symbolize them.

As the props begin to arrive in the rehearsal hall, and they should come no later than the second time the actors are off book in the scenes that contain them, most of these props will be mock-ups. You should encourage your actors to give props an independent life through their imagination and images. Just as the actor has relationships with characters and furniture in the play, they should have a backstory for the vase and figurine on the coffee table as well.

Actors should have an attitude associated with every object they handle. Where did it come from? How long has it been there? How did it get that chip or dent? The stronger the actor has created their backstory, the more confidence and comfort they will feel; the stronger the objects speak to the actor, the more creative choices they will make with their props.

Once actors endow their props and furniture with a backstory, these objects become supporting characters in the play. If your actors have not worked with this process in the past, encourage them to commit their imaginations to it.

The character does not have to live in the play's' setting to benefit from object relationships. The following is a recollection by the American actor Morris Carnovsky, a distinguished member of the Group Theatre, as he describes his role as a character entering a home that he does not live in but has occasionally visited:

"I was playing some years ago in *An Enemy of the People* … I was playing the brother of Dr. Stockman [...]. When I come in, when I took off my hat, deposited my umbrella in the areaway where I come in, to relate to things, here is my hat, it is my hat. This is that lamp, that expensive lamp my foolish brother bought. Here is a tablecloth. I do not have any such tablecloth in my house. This carpet is probably much finer than anything anybody in town has. [...] Already, this began to induce me to enter into the life of the play and through simple objects. So that all at once I felt at home. Even though I was criticizing these surroundings, it was the place where I had to act. Therefore, these things reassured me; so that when I sat down on a chair, a too expensive chair by the way … I already had an attitude, to the whole room, and everybody in it. So, that the animosity which then proceeded to be expressed started from simple ordinary objects, which reassured my being, being me, Morris Carnovsky's being within the character."

Exercise #11

As If's and Like

As if's are figurative comparisons to aid an actor's discovery. Let us say you are working with an actress whose character has had a shock and is about to faint. She has gone blank on how to proceed. You might suggest the image: "You are light, like as a feather in a cold wind." Hopefully she would let her senses explore texture, temperature, and weight, experiencing the physical sensations suggested in the figures of speech. For an actor needing help playing a witness in court caught in a lie, you might say, "It's as if you are a young child caught stealing cookies from a jar."

Exercise #12

Stop, Image, Text

Your actors are speaking, but their imaginations are not active; what do you do? Rather than yelling "I don't believe you," say, "*Stop-image.*" They pause for an instant, and then give a summary, describing a personal experience. They respond, "That time with my father in the kitchen." Then you say, "Repeat the line with that image please." If the actors choose a vivid image, they rekindle their connection to the text. Their imaginations are active again, belief in the moment is recreated, then you simply say text and they continue with the dialogue. They proceed until the next tentative moment in the scene needing more specificity and you repeat *stop-image*.

If their responses are not stimulating them, suggest sense images by saying, "What do you see, touch, taste, smell, and hear?" If they continue to have difficulty finding personal images, ask them to use their daydreams, what they might fantasize to do in the characters' *given circumstances.* When you see images forming in your actor's eyes, say "text," and let the rehearsal continue until the next trouble spot.

Perhaps as you read the stop, image, text, you are wondering why the actor's description of their image needs to be so elliptical, almost as if they are in code. The director says, "image" and the actor replied, "that time in the kitchen when my father." Doesn't the director want more information? The answer is no. You require no more specificity, and furthermore, you should not have it. The actor says a few vivid words, but it is enough to spark stimulus in their mind and body. Further details of an actor's image are unnecessary, and frankly, nobody's business but their own. Images are flickers of the actor's private life. Your only job is to help them turn on their power source and keep the light on.

This technique clears up problems in stop-and-go rehearsals. You should at the outset explain the procedure of *Stop, Image, Text* so the actors understand the objective of it. At the end of successful work, congratulate them on their accomplishments and then do a nonstop run-through of the same material. When the actors sense tangible improvement, morale builds in the company.

Expect there to be ups and downs in the work. Rehearsals tend to vary, much like temperature. Work diligently to keep your irritations under control. Avoid chastising your actors with negative outbursts. Avoid statements like, "What is the problem here? Yesterday this was starting to come together and now you're forgetting all the new work we did." Such statements only foster insecurity and likely resentment among your actors. Strive to avoid the negative. Be sensitive to their learning curve. Tailor your rehearsal schedule accordingly, and the opportunity for a productive and creative process will increase. One of the wisest axioms of directing is: For all the time you spend taking the text apart, spend an equal amount putting it back together. Directors too frequently give more emphasis to the former than the latter.

In a run-through of a unit, be specific in your note-taking. If you don't believe a moment because the actor seemed to lack any stimulus under a line, write down the specific words so you can work with them later on that moment. Give your actors a short break after the completion of a scene, act, or run through so you can review your notes and write additional observations.

Offer praise for particular sections of the text that are progressing. Do not, however, in your praise describe a moment or *physical action* the actor performs by saying, "I loved that bit you had of fumbling with your ring when you put down the cup." By specifically describing an event that was spontaneous for the actor, you run the risk of making them self-conscious of it. It may be impossible for them to make it as spontaneous again; praise in general, not about specific actions. If you see there is a tendency for an actor to excessively play to the audience, give them a note to share their image with their partners.

Encourage actors to do their image homework. It is unlikely that it will all happen in rehearsals. Personal images of emotional memories and fantasy images will need more preparation outside of rehearsals.

Don't let your cast discover their images on the floor. Sometimes actors, through insecurity or getting lost in their imaginary world, tend to lower their heads in key moments that need to be shared with their partners or the audience. A fascination with the floor creates an audibility problem, as well as losing the actors ever-important eyes.

Be aware of the proper placement of images. Avoid actors playing shared personal imagery, too close to one another. In intense moments, the emphasis should be on partner connections, more than their images. Strong images need space. Actors in realistic plays may need to extend their fourth wall beyond the stage apron. Acting coach Uta Hagen suggested actors place imaginary fourth wall windows over exit signs, balcony rails, and other locations in the theatre house to extend their imaginary environment and thus increase the accessibility of their images.

Counsel your actors not to panic if a favorite image goes blank from overuse. It can happen rather frequently. New images need to be created when established ones fade. Often the original one will return in later rehearsals or the run of the show.

Outdoor scenic locations provide actors the opportunity of opening up to three-quarters or full-front body positions, particularly as their character's deal with the environment, such as looking at landscapes. Images here need to be as vivid and specific as possible. There have been moments in theatre productions when audience members have turned around in their seats to see what created the actor's apparent fascination with the view behind them. Actors need to work on powerful images that might evoke that kind of response.

Be cautious in plays of realism set indoors of the overuse of full front body positions, in moments of powerful actor imagery. Because it is highly dramatic, directors tend to overuse it. Actors downstage have only windows to motivate an outward gaze. Actors upstage may play scenes of intense personal imagery full front, to downstage partners, but if they are too far away from them, they lose intimacy. Most scenes require more muted three-quarter open body positions.

In classical plays, especially Shakespeare, asides and soliloquies are usually played directly to the audience. You need to help your actors make choices whether they are placing images just over the heads of audience members or are making direct eye contact with them. If it is direct, is the character speaking to the present audience member? Or are they using the picture of someone else and substituting the spectator for them? Or are they creating a substitution of a real person in their life, their sister, fifth-grade teacher, or college roommate?

The legendary English actor Sir Ralph Richardson was once asked by an eager young reporter, "Sir Ralph, in a brief statement can you define the secret of remarkable acting?" Without hesitation Richardson responded, "Wind and dreams." That is perhaps the most concise definition of acting ever recorded. Richardson demonstrated profound insight in suggesting the power of the interaction of breath and image is integral to a successful acting process.

In the next chapter, I will explore the important concept of actors *Playing Together* in concentration, connection, and vulnerability.

7

Playing Together

The term "ensemble production" is among the highest compliments offered to a director's work. It suggests a play with a group dedication in which individual egos merge to serve the author's text. It doesn't occur by chance. It must be carefully nurtured.

I'm not suggesting that actors untamed are unbridled egotists out to steal every scene, dominate the stage, and keep their partners in the shadows. When we see actors not connecting with one another, acting alone, it is more often a sign of insecurity than megalomania. Acting is a courageous profession because it demands complete, exposed vulnerability before an audience of total strangers.

It is little wonder then, given these demands, that actors often feel such extreme insecurity. They may consider their only option is to act alone relying on their strengths. This is detrimental to their performance, but the impulse is understandable. When actors shut out their partners, and act alone, the director must share in their failure.

It is our job to create an atmosphere in rehearsals where mutual openness, trust, and interdependence exist. This is why I earlier suggested that time should be spent in the exploratory rehearsals working on ensemble and trust exercises such as *Sending the Spark*, *The Silent Gift, and Living Entity*, among others.

Actors are as dependent upon each other as aerialists, who must rely on each other to survive, high above an awestruck crowd, holding absolute concentration upon which their lives depend. Actors' artistic lives in a production are equally dependent on their relationship as SENDERS and RECEIVERS. The communication process in acting consists of a partner sending a stream of energy to another actor. That energy lands on the partner—it hits them—they physically receive it—discover their reactions to it and send a new stream of energy back. This is ensemble acting. It is the director coach's highest priority to nourish this process.

This chapter focuses on *Polishing Rehearsals,* dealing with in-depth coaching when actors are off-book. It consists of fourteen exercises and games to help you build an acting ensemble. They are divided into three categories of common actor problems and deal with the most recurring actor challenges: CONCENTRATION, CONNECTION, and VULNERABILITY. You will discover they have broader applications beyond these categories and will serve you in solving any number of actor needs.

These exercises are geared to produce positive outcomes within a brief time frame. You should have the confidence to stop any rehearsal to apply them, knowing you have possible solutions to your actor's problems.

I CONCENTRATION

Exercise #1
The Psychic Circle

This is an exercise adapted from the masterful director actor-coach Michael Chekhov from his book *To the Actor,* which builds trust and concentration. Work in groups of three to eight actors until the entire cast has experienced the exercise.

Ask them to stand in a circle facing one another. Suggest to them they are professional psychics with the powers of extrasensory perception. Their task is to read one another's' minds and consent on a given count, by executing a simple physical action in unison. To accomplish this, they will agree upon a gesture and perform it simultaneously. Give your "psychics" three simple physical actions to choose from. For example: one, raise your left arm; two, raise your right arm; three, extend both arms in front of you. Explain that you will count slowly to twenty. They will then demonstrate the group choice as they execute the correct gesture together. Start the count and ask them to be completely open to one another.

Have each member establish eye contact with each other, mentally projecting goodwill, making a silent promise to work positively together to achieve their goal. Each actor will then send their ESP rays to communicate which gesture the entire group will perform. Caution them not to cheat by telegraphing body language that gives away their choice. Keep them to the goal of projecting positive energy that says, "Please join me in performing action number one, two or three on the count of twenty." Ask the group to project thoughts of, "Let's perform this action together." Avoid the coercion of, "You will accept my choice." At about mid-count, the group should switch from *sending* to *receiving*. Each circle member again continues close eye contact with one another to receive the group choice. The director slows down the count as they proceed. When they reach twenty, the circle immediately performs their action.

You will likely be surprised at the, nearly complete, unanimity of the group. If, as occasionally happens, there is wide diversity in the execution of the three actions, repeat the exercise so the cast may work for greater concentration.

While it is fun for the actors to think in imagery of ESP and invisible rays, the experience is not so much mystical as it is a metaphorical representation of the acting process. It is the act of actors *sending* and *receiving* energies to create a vital ensemble. This exercise may be applied as early as the exploratory rehearsal period. It is, however, even more, pertinent here, as the actors must now in polishing rehearsals sense the necessity of relying on their partners to receive, acknowledge, and return their responses to the energy sent.

Exercise # 2

A Secret Message Decoded

This game can strengthen and empower the two actors' relationship. Gibberish or invented language, is often employed by coaching directors in exercises and improvs because it forces actors to exert greater concentration in working with their partners. The sense of secrecy in this exercise helps create a bonding relationship between actors through it's, "this is for your ears only", tone. Gibberish secrets are helpful because the partners they will "translate" each other's coded stories, and deepen their concentration.

You begin this game by asking two actors to sit close together, facing one another. Each will share a short truthful anecdote about the pleasures or problems that they are experiencing with their role or a related rehearsal experience. Rather than speaking English, they share their thoughts in gibberish. This may be any combination of vowels and consonants that the actors will invent. You do need to caution them to avoid any excessive physical actions that would make the story instantly obvious. The incident should be approximately one minute or less, otherwise the partner may experience difficulty translating. When the anecdote is concluded, the other actor will immediately interpret it in English. They will then offer their own gibberish story for their partner to decode.

This game is not as difficult as it may sound. I have often seen actors interpret gibberish messages with near-absolute accuracy; they almost always get at least the general idea of the story. Complete accuracy is not the point. What is of importance here is establishing a deeper level of teamwork and support. The actors' discoveries from this gibberish game can lead to new trust and rapport as they take pleasure in breaking down each other's language barriers.

Exercise #3

Conversations in the Dark

This exercise is designed for actors who are off book for a scene that is yet to come alive. The objective is to heighten their level of concentration and provide them with sensory awareness. It works well with either two actors or a group ensemble scene.

It should ideally take place in a comfortable space that can be darkened. The actors should sit close together on the floor, facing their partner(s). In a welcoming state, they will breathe deeply, looking into each other's eyes. They should establish silent mutual acceptance for about fifteen seconds. Now they should separate and move a few feet apart, lying on their backs in a relaxed position.

At this point, you will turn off the lights in the room so it is in complete darkness. Now, request them to use their visual imaginations to create a picture of their partners' faces that they have just observed in the light. Ask them to get in touch with their other senses in this darkened room. What sounds do they hear? Do they detect any odors? Is it cool or warm?

With their senses alive, ask them to begin speaking the words of the scene to each other, but much slower than they have previously rehearsed. Request your actors to hear each word their partners utter with a new importance, as if experiencing it for the first time. You may need to urge them to slow down further and work for total comfort and relaxation. You are inviting them to be on the verge of drifting into sleep but challenging them in this state, to send their words with enough energy to directly connect with their partner. Ask the receiving partners to be impacted by these words. The new element of the dark will offer them different perceptions of the scene. They should experience a higher level of listening and more sustained concentration, which will result in new acting choices.

If the scene is of a moderate length of three to five minutes, run the entire scene in this manner. If it is longer, I would suggest breaking it at this point. Restore the lights and ask your actors to run the scene nonstop with their blocking at its intended tempo.

At the conclusion, let them comment on their experience with the exercise, then offer your evaluation. It has been my experience that actors enjoy this conversation in the dark, and the results frequently yield signs of new life in a static scene.

Exercise #4
Sender/Receiver

Since the chapter on Exploratory Rehearsals, I have been urging you to be certain that your actors are *sending and receiving* impulses together. This begins to happen when an actor senses the amount of breath and energy required to reach their partner. Often in rehearsals, and unfortunately in performances as well, an actor may aim a line in the direction of their intended partner, but it falls to the floor between them before it reaches its target. When this occurs, communication breaks down and the play's story begins to lose focus.

The audience becomes confused if the actors continue to disconnect. They become distracted, then bored and ultimately lose interest in the story. The coaching director must come to the aid of their actors. You will be their referee and offer them these games to master the concept of *sending and receiving*. For those actors having problems with this process, coaching should begin earlier than polishing rehearsals. As soon as actors are off book and experience connection problems, a game of Sender/Receiver should help them establish improved concentration. Ask your actors to stand approximately six to eight feet apart facing one another. To warm up, they will toss a variety of imaginary balls to each other. The sender may start by throwing a softball, which the receiver mimes receiving and returns. On the senders' next toss, they may change it into a light beach ball, football, basketball, tennis, or rubber ball. You will serve as the referee calling each play. If you judge the same ball that was received that was sent, you call, "transform." If the exchange doesn't seem accurate, if it appears, for instance, that a softball was thrown and a rubber one was caught, you call, "Repeat."

Within a brief period the concentration of the partners should be heightened. Your calls may occasionally be wrong. What referee in the history of sport has a perfect record? You will judge by observing the same clues that your actors should. That is, the size of the ball, the actor's handling of its texture, its weight, and the energy required in throwing it as well as their overall body language in relation to it.

With the warm-up completed, your actors are ready to play the game using the dialogue of the text; they will continue to mime both the throw and the catch in a tempo slower than they will play it in performance. The sender chooses an imaginary ball of the size and weight that might coincide with the quality of the line spoken. A casual tennis ball toss, for instance, may be perfect for a comic throwaway line, while a basketball could be an appropriate choice for a powerful, emotional revelation. The sender may or may not choose to change the kind of imaginary ball on each line. The receiver must not drop it and must closely observe the pitcher to see and accurately receive the type of ball thrown.

The great value of this game is that it builds concentration and connection between the actors and allows them to physicalize their feelings of the play's dialogue.

II. CONNECTION

Exercise #5
Blind and Sighted

Set up a working space with several physical obstacles in it such as chairs, stools, ladders, screens, etc. Or you may wish to use the mock-up furniture on your ground plan. Have your actors work in pairs, designating one the sighted partner, the other the "blind" actor who closes or covers their eyes. The objective is for the seeing actor to lead the "blind" one through this maze, slowly leading them with their hand, then increasing the speed. As the "blind" partner's security grows, they should grasp only the seeing actor's fingertips.

As confidence builds, the sighted partner creates more obstacles in the maze by moving through varying levels, as they lead the partner to step on stools, climb ladders, or crawl on the floor and around barriers. The sighted actor must take extreme care to protect their partner from stumbling, colliding with objects, or if it is a group exercise, banging into one another. The leader is working to help the "blind" partner be as venturesome as possible while constantly aware of their tenuous position.

The sighted actor gains a sense of responsibility and concern for their partner that is at the heart of a strong acting ensemble. They may imagine that it is as if their "blind" partner is the last precious statue on earth; one false move and they may shatter to dust. After a suitable workout, the partners will exchange roles.

Exercise #6

A Mile in His Moccasins

You have likely heard the Native American adage, "You don't know a person until you have walked a mile in their moccasins." This is valuable advice for actors because they need to try to understand the motives and feelings of all the characters in the play with whom they interact.

When the actors understand their partner's character impulses, deeper, more powerful choices will emerge in their relationships. If an arc of a play moves from friendship and culminates in love and then marriage, both actors should understand each other's intentions and feelings at each step in their journey. Conversely, characters locked in antagonistic relationships will gain insight when they understand their opponents' needs and their will to succeed. They will then be able to counter with their *psychological actions*, in hopes of overcoming the *obstacles* imposed on them. The goal for actors here is in their developing empathy, vicariously *experiencing* the feelings, thoughts, and attitudes of the other characters, so that they may develop better strategies with them.

Your actors can achieve empathy when they engage in switching roles. You should choose a scene in which you want them to strengthen a relationship. Gender is irrelevant here. Request your actors to reverse their roles and read the scene. At the conclusion, ask them if their characters perceptions changed or new discoveries were made.

You might ask them to continue the role reversal in an improv you structure from the play that is relevant to their relationship. As always, return to the original casting and run the scene again. Hopefully, both actors will emerge with a stronger sense of their partners' world.

Exercise #7

Long-Distance Connection

Here is another exercise that builds actor connection and listening skills. Think how intensely we listen on the telephone in a conversation with a friend or loved one over the distance of another state or country. We may be in awe of the miles that separate us or the technology that makes it possible; our concentration is generally powerful. Use the image of a long-distance connection as another approach to aid actors who need to improve their connection in a scene.

Have your actors sit in chairs or the floor on opposite sides of the rehearsal space with their backs to one another. They have previously shared each other's actual cell phone numbers and now with their phones in hand one actor dials the other and the phone rings. The actors will speak the dialogue of a scene as if it were an overseas call.

As the conversation begins, they should each visualize their partner as their initial image. Ask your actors to apply "the illusion of the first time." It should be as if they have never spoken these words or heard their partner speak theirs. Suggest, as an *obstacle*, that the connection isn't perfect, and they have to carefully concentrate to hear the other's words. Despite this slight impediment, the tone should be conversational with the increased excitement of connecting over a great distance. Allow the phone call to progress for several minutes. As the scene builds, ask both actors to continue the conversation. Then, request them to rise, turn to face each other, and slowly move into the blocking of the scene. They should then put their cell phones in their pockets and continue to play the circumstances of the text. Because this situation deals with a reality, the actors have likely experienced, there is a strong probability that this exercise may break open the scene and create a new life that previously was lacking

Exercise #8
Exploring New Territory

A relatively common problem, as a production enters its final stages, is a scene that has been run many times loses its spontaneity, and staleness creeps into the work. The actors, without quite realizing it, are playing on autopilot, not talking or listening to each other, lacking their original connection. This exercise brings actors back to the reality of the moment.

As you begin the scene, direct the actors to change their blocking. For example, if it is a scene of some intimacy in which two actors have been placed close to each other, direct one character to move as far away from their partner as the space permits. Ask them now to begin the scene, working to preserve the original intent of emotional closeness. The dynamic of the scene will, of course, change. The actors will need to adjust their energy levels to reach each other as they simultaneously strive to retain the intimacy inherent in the script. This *obstacle* should jolt the actors' concentration levels and guide them to work together again. This exercise intends to turn the original blocking topsy-turvy. If you have a scene where two characters are far apart because their emotional relationship is strained, ask your actors to play it face to face.

They must stay in the world of the play, but work to adapt their characters to these new spatial challenges. Because these changing physical circumstances are so different than the previously established blocking, the actors will need to channel all their resources toward each other to keep the scene truthful.

As in all the exercises, but especially here, where circumstances or blocking has been altered as a coaching technique, be sure to return to the original staging immediately after the end of the exercise so the sense of discovery or, in this case, re-discovery may occur.

Exercise #9

Gumdrop Darts

This game, like the last, has the same objective of building power through connection. It is a favorite of mine because it manages to both problem-solve and be highly entertaining for the actors to perform. Additionally, it leads them to understand the importance of *follow-through*, the partner's reaction to what was just said. Follow-through is often crucial to the audience's understanding of what just happened from moment to moment in the play.

The fun for the actors in this game is the comic idea that they have an unlimited number of imaginary darts. Secured to the dart's point is a sugary gumdrop. Each actor speaks their dialogue, aiming their dart at their partner's forehead, just above their eyes. They physicalize throwing it on each line of dialogue. If either partner feels that the dart does not stick, or it lands anywhere other than where it was intended, the actor must aim again, repeat their line, and throw it to connect with their partner, as eye contact is maintained.

You may want to referee and call a hit or a miss, or you may allow the actors to make their judgments. If either actor judges that the target was missed, they should raise their arm to signify a pause. The dart holder will then try again to hit their partner's forehead, with the gummy missile, as they speak their line.

The actors should work with approximately two minutes of memorized text, moving through their established blocking. They will begin speaking slowly; holding an imaginary dart, they will aim, and on a keyword, throw it to connect with their partner's forehead.

The partner pauses after they have received the gumdrop blow. This reaction should be physicalized as well, but not an over-played reaction, rather, a simple sensory awareness that the dart has hit their brow. In a brief pause, the actor decides on a tactical response. This is the process of *follow-through* and should last only a second.

Compliment your actors to the degree they were successful in their first round. It will be helpful now to discuss what they achieved. You might ask: Was there sustained eye contact between you? Did each of you have sufficient breath support to achieve ease and clarity of speech? Was your energy level appropriate to the words you spoke? Could you see in your partner's eyes, an inner image working?

Continue till the actors have ease with the process. Then explain none of the physical throwing actions will be required in the next round. This time in the scene, the gumdrop darts should become only an inner mental image that the characters are sharing.

The game is now more of a traditional run-through, although it should still move more slowly, so the actors can savor the action and time their speeches with the impact of the darts hitting their partners' foreheads.

III. VULNERABILITY

Exercise #10
Help me

This improv was developed by the distinguished American director and acting coach Joseph Anthony. It can have a strong bonding effect among actors and is particularly effective with larger casts. It can be especially helpful in the early rehearsals.

Divide the company into two equal groups. Ask them to stand in two lines about eight to ten feet apart, directly facing one another. Tell your cast to establish eye contact with their counterpart in the opposite group. The director will give opposing objectives to each unit. The instructions are private and not to be shared with the other group. Surprise is essential to the improv.

Whisper to one group that they are in dire circumstances that they will imagine for themselves. The stakes are life and death; each actor in the distracted group, is dependent on the person they face in the opposite group to save them. As the improv begins, they will establish eye contact, and with their last hope for survival, extend their arms in supplication and utter the words, "Help me." Before this action begins, you will have privately told the other group to resist all pleas for assistance. Each individual in this line must be stone-faced and unyielding. Despite the desperate pleas of their counterpart, they stare back in cold silence.

With these circumstances clear, the needful characters repeat the plea, "help me," as they confront the critical silent ones. You should allow this encounter to continue close to a minute at a total impasse. Then build tension by asking the suppliant group to continue speaking and move one step toward their mute, unresponsive partners, then a second step, then a third. They hold there and repeat their plea, "help me." The two groups should now be only a few feet apart. As the tension seems unbearable, clap your hands; turn to the resisting group, and tell them "to run to their partners. Embrace them, help them, revive them."

After a moment of shock, there will likely be extended embraces, deep sighs, and perhaps some tears from the one group, and smiles, satisfaction, and pleasure from the other. This powerfully cathartic experience will begin to build a bonded acting ensemble, open and available to one another.

Exercise #11
They're Playing Our Song

You are aware of the power of music in a theatre production. An incisive selection of pre-show music can immediately pull your audience into the moods and emotions of a play. Music can have the same effect on your actors in rehearsals. It can open up a scene and touch them with new and powerful feelings. Silent film actors were surrounded by live musicians playing music the director thought appropriate as the cameras rolled. Modern coaching directors can give that old practice a new twist with this exercise.

When you are working on a scene of a budding romance or an intense love sequence, if your actors are having difficulties responding to the text or each other, ask them, "to find their song." A day before you plan to use this technique, request both actors confer and try to discover a piece of music they both can associate with the emotions of their scene and bring a recording of it to the next rehearsal.

Now, play the music and ask them to freely associate it with their feelings in the scene. They should travel in their imagination where the music takes them. Then, with the actors seated, repeat the song, at a low level, underscoring it, as the actors run their dialogue.

The next step is for the actors to rise and begin to dance to the music as they speak their lines. If the song is an earlier American standard, the actors can dance in the traditional ballroom styles. If the music is contemporary, they should improvise their movement. Whatever the style, the partners need to keep a close, physical connection throughout the dance.

As they relax into the music and dance while speaking their lines, they will discover new connections with each other. You may need to side coach your actors in the dance to retain eye contact with each other and keep moving.

Ask the actors now to return to a traditional rehearsal, using the pre-established blocking of the scene. Suggest that they use the memory of the music and the kinetic sense of their connection in the dance as inner images. At the conclusion, offer your actors notes on what you saw and where the scene needs to go from here. Music as a coaching technique has broad applications with different music styles matching different genres of plays.

Exercise #12
Relive the Love

This vulnerability improv leads your actors to discover or rediscover an essential ingredient in their character relationships, which is, the love they share.

I am speaking not only of romantic scenes, but also intense family conflicts that end in reconciliation, or character relationships that on the surface may appear hurtful, but sub-textually are driven by love. Casting director Michael Shurtleff, in his book *Audition*, states that "every scene is a love scene on some level." You should ask your actors to identify the source of their love and then connect with it.

This improv is geared to either deepen the love in a scene or to re-discover it if it has faded during rehearsals and your actors now need a shot of adrenaline. It may be approached either silently or with minimal dialogue. The participants will be at the center stage. Ask them to stand a few feet apart facing each other with strong eye contact. They are saying goodbye to one another with the realization they may never meet again. They will first warmly embrace.

As they continue visual contact, they will slowly take a few backward steps away from one another, keeping an intense focus on their partner's eyes. This strong momentary visual connection, will be either silent or with brief words, as the emotional circumstances of their separation affects them. Now you will ask them to turn away from each other and cross in opposite directions to the right and left far edges of the acting space. They then pause. Their eyes should close for approximately fifteen to thirty seconds. In this time, they will envision a passage of months or perhaps years of separation. Now, tell them they will have a joyful reunion with their loved one. They should turn, rush to, embrace one another and fully experience their unexpected happiness together. Give them some time to be fully in touch with this emotional event. Urge your actors to work to retain these feelings, and access them again in rehearsal and performance.

Exercise # 13

When I was a Little Girl or Boy

This exercise was used with success by actor coach and director Jack Clay. With this experience, actors will open themselves up emotionally and become more accessible to their partners.

Have your actors sit in chairs and establish eye contact. This is a personal recall technique that resembles emotional memory. Rather than selecting a single memory, the participants share with their partners a sustained series of unedited experiences, both happy and sad from their early years of life. The actors will speak the phrases, "When I was a little girl," or, "When I was a little boy."

The phrase, "When I was a little …" repeats with each new event following in rapid succession, to ensure spontaneity. The exercise demands the quick recall of as many truthful personal childhood memories as possible. Experiences from their earliest recollection to near adolescence are the most effective. The actors should work freely to verbalize the first impressions that enter their minds. Each partner should relate their entire story before the other speaks.

You may need to side coach with encouragement by remarking, "Yes, good, more, keep going." Urge the participants to sustain a steady conversation that ideally should extend for several minutes. At the outset, suggesting that the actors search for contrasting events in their childhood from playfulness to cruelty as, "When I was a little girl, after it rained, I went to the backyard and baked mud pies." Or, "When I was a little boy, I pulled the wings off of flies."

As each actor lets down their barriers, sharing private experiences, there tends to be a flood of memories that will likely run from tearful to hilarious. It is not unusual for the exercise to end with the actors choked on laughter or with tears streaming down their faces, or both. By sharing vulnerable stories, any inhibitions the partners may have felt with each other should disappear. This can be a perfect moment to pursue challenging, emotional material in the text.

Exercise #14
Infants at Play

This is an exercise that solves a variety of actor challenges. It is invariably entertaining for the actors who engage in it, a comic diversion in rehearsals for those who observe it, and almost always a reliable solution.

The premise of the exercise is that your actors cast off their adult selves and enter again into the world of childhood. They engage in the *given circumstances* of their scene with the spontaneous, innocence of small infants. They lack language skills and will speak in a kind of nonsense baby gibberish of mostly single syllables. What is the purpose of such an exercise? Quite simply, it is to aid those actors who are struggling with common problems such as lack of emotional availability or discomfort with a partner. It allows them to free themselves from adult limitations and open up to the visceral, uncensored behavior of infants. Infancy and vulnerability are synonymous.

To begin, explain to your actors that they will work on the scene moving through their established blocking as if they were babies. The obstacles are their limited mental capabilities and language skills. They will communicate through baby monosyllables, such as: ga, goo, da, dee, doe.

The objective is to play the content of the scene in baby gibberish. To accomplish this, they will have an ongoing inner monologue of the scenes dialogue that they are translating into baby talk. This will happen automatically when the actors are solid in their lines. I have never witnessed a rendering of this exercise when the "infants" were at a loss for speech.

Your actors will begin the scene as blank slates, and will learn from each new life incident in the script, which they will magnify to extremes; hurt, delight, rage, love, or jealousy, which may explode with the frequency of a string of lighted firecrackers as they alternate between laughter and tears.

The key to the success of the exercise is for the actors to release themselves into the world of comedy. The idea of infants dealing with adult issues of which they are entirely ignorant is inherently comic. Your actors should not aim, however, to play a comedy sketch or mockery of childhood. Rather, they should allow themselves to enter into a state of innocent childish behavior in which they become overwhelmed by their circumstances. They should experience a sense of initial wonder in everything they do. Encourage your actors to be tactile. They should find impulses to touch props as well as each other on every line possible. There are no social inhibitions for one-year-olds.

If you have chosen this exercise because of your actors' tentativeness or unresponsiveness to each other, it is likely to drop away as they enter their infantile state. A sense of delight and innate silliness should give them the impetus they need to connect in the scene; their foolishness releases barriers that will lead to new discoveries and growth in their work.

Infants at Play can be useful in love scenes as well as moments of intense scrutiny when characters are seeking out each other's motives. It will be helpful in scenes of anger, or volatility, characterized by sudden mood swings, moments of quick beat changes resulting in highly contrasting emotions. Are these situations not similar to vulnerable infants who, free from social conventions, may explode into temper tantrums with one another that momentarily turn into pure adoring bliss?

As you engage in this exercise, I would urge you to enjoy the laughter and allow your actors and other cast members to do likewise. Laughter is a revitalizing tonic in the rehearsal process. Comedy may well be the catalyst that takes serious material to a new level of excellence. This exercise was the creation of Constance Welch, a famed acting teacher at the Yale Drama School from the 1920s to the 1960s, and it comes to you well tested.

8

Psychophysical Solo Coaching

The term psycho physical-action may be familiar to you. Its origin is in Stanislavsky's "theory of physical actions," a late discovery which he describes in his final book, "*Creating a Role*." He tells us he was abandoning the long hours at the table, involved in character discussions, and instead of using *physical actions* as his first stage of character development. He suggests, "feeling follows action in a part{…}so why not coach it from the very start {…}why sit at a table for months and try to force out your dormant feelings {…} you would do better to go out on the stage and at once engage in action." The following exercises will be of importance to your actors from the earliest rehearsals. I introduce them here because they demonstrate how psycho-physical actions lead the actor to feelings that are truthful and allow for maximum physical freedom.

Exercise #1
The Wall

One of the most common problems for beginning or anxiety-burdened actors is a lack of physicality in their role, demonstrated by low energy. The observant director will diagnose this as a lack of spine involvement, figuratively and literally, actors lacking backbone in their acting. Suggest to those actors the following physical activities. Using a memorized speech, they move to a wall and establish a wide base with their feet, placing their outstretched palms against the wall. Next, request that they take a deep breath, exhale, and speak the first line of their dialogue, pushing firmly against the wall. Then they will continue the dialogue while pushing.

You should monitor their breathing. Be certain they inhale deeply and do not hold their breath. They should continue the dialogue as they push against the wall on each line. When their power and energy have increased, ask them to stop. Now request them to experience in their body the physical action of the sensation of pushing the wall. Give them a moment to do this. They should now face you and repeat their lines with the circumstances of the scene, without the literal push.

Exercise #2
Palm to Palm Power

It may be helpful for some of your actors, lacking necessary energy, in a scene to participate in a more sustained variation of the preceding WALL exercise. If the problem is limited to only a single cast member, this should be a private coaching session. If you are encountering several actors with low unfocused energy, you should stop the rehearsal to work with the entire cast on this challenge.

Ask the actors to choose a partner. Standing close together they should place their hands vertically on each other's palms. The first step will be the same as in the last exercise, using the dialog of a duo scene. One actor is the pusher, the other the "wall." The pusher, with the same energy level they have been using in the rehearsals, will apply pressure, palm to palm against the "wall" actor. Allow the action to continue for several lines for both actors, with the wall solidly resisting. They will realize they are straining to break through an impasse, but are not properly connecting, which may be their problems in rehearsals as well. Suggest to them now that they begin again palm to palm, gently pushing back and forth, sensing the rhythm of the lines. Ask them to sustain the dialogue as they maintain the continuous touch. As they begin to relax, ask that one actor begins to slowly rock their body from toe to heel. The partner then picks up on this action and does likewise. They should have the feeling of being on a child's teeter-totter. Allow this rocking to continue as you see their comfort growing. Then softly say to them, "now begin to walk moving palm to palm, continuing to speak your dialogue." Let this continue until you sense their comfort with the exercise. Compliment them and ask them to retain their discoveries as they return to play the scene as blocked. Greater relaxation, power, and connection should be your actor's rewards and for you the coaching director, visual proof that, "feelings follow actions."

Exercise #3
Physical Sports

Actors can make remarkable discoveries when they learn that entering into physical actions associated with sports activities can bring clarity to difficult passages in a script and help them engage physically in their role.

If an actor, frustrated by a challenging passage says, "I just can't get the *feel* of it," that is your cue to help them find meaning through physicalization. The intended sense of the dialogue will often become clearer and more filled when an actor executes the actions of a physical sport while speaking their dialogue. The actions should match the intensity and stamina needed to play the actual sport and it should be similar to the mood and rhythm of the scene. The actor will discover new stresses, rhythms, and ranges of emotions in the lines that will lead to a greater clarity of the script.

Their physical action should be common physical sports activities such as: pitching a ball, throwing darts, bowling, or kicking a soccer ball. Have the actor begin the physical actions of the sport with the dialogue much slower than the scene will be played. This initial investigative process may be in slow motion, both verbally and physically. Gradually, the actor brings it up to the proper tempo. They now accept the imaginary circumstance, that the sports activity is continuous. That is, for example, as soon as they release a bowling ball down the lane, another appears in their hand, so the physical activity will be sustained to coincide with the length and phrasing of a spoken line.

Much of the success of the exercise will depend on the actor's skill and yours in matching the rhythm of their textual line to the corresponding rhythm of a specific sport's action. A slow swimming stroke, for instance, it may be well suited to a languid line of text, whereas dribbling and shooting a basketball would be appropriate for dialogue with a staccato dynamic quality.

To put your actors more at ease, recommend that they choose a sport they know well, perhaps one they play or have played. As they coordinate dialogue with the physical action, the inherent wisdom of the body kicks in and the appropriate stress, phrasing, and flow of the language tends to follow.

I would urge you to try this exercise yourself. You might select a Shakespeare passage. Read it over silently; decide on what physical sport might be appropriate for the piece and then simultaneously physicalize and vocalize it. This exercise should be experienced to be fully appreciated.

Another valuable application for *Physical Sports* is using it as a full company exercise when you begin work on a verse play. It can prove most valuable for players working on Shakespeare. You may wish to use it through several scenes in rehearsals.

Also, you can apply the *Physical Sport* movement as an exercise to build the *actor's deeper commitment in a scene.* For example, in choosing Shakespeare's most well-known soliloquy, *Hamlet's,* "To be or not to be," your actor might choose the physical sport of rowing.

Hamlet, contemplating suicide, is in a small rowboat on a Denmark lake. He starts from shore speaking, "To be. ..." He intends to row toward mid-lake where he plans to drown himself. His oars will be crucial. They will be functional as the actor mimes them slowly and expansively to connect with the verse and the reality of the situation. He stops rowing after he verbalizes, "Thus conscience doth make cowards of us all," and the boat floats on the line "And lose the name of action." He takes a long contemplative pause; with the oars, he turns the boat around and heads for shore.

Physical Sports can serve as a powerful trigger to help open up previously obscure passages, take them in new directions emotionally, and more fully convey the language and meaning of the play.

Exercise #4
Shakespeare Acrobatic

This is a variation on the preceding exercise of *Physical Sports*. Both of these techniques were developed by Constance Welch at the Yale Drama School. The principle again uses physical movement to discover both rhythm and meaning in a scene. While the title suggests the exercise is geared to Shakespeare plays, it is suitable and has proved highly effective in working with all periods and genres of poetic texts. Do not be put off by the term acrobatic. I am not suggesting that your actors become trapeze artists or contortionists, rather, the actors should use their creativity in this free form exercise.

Unlike the preceding *Physical Sports* exercise, where there are rules of the game, here you are asking the actor to spontaneously create their own choreography. Shakespeare will be their guide. Remember Hamlet's advice to the actors, "Suit the word to the action and the action to the word." As your actor speaks the playwright's language, they move to the rhythms, ideas, and feelings of their words, as they use their bodies to interpret the text. Again, feeling follows action.

There is total freedom here for the actors as you encourage them to use their own physical vocabulary. Actors with little or no dance training can have a breakthrough with this exercise. Any genre from ballet to hip-hop, using improvised movements, can be effective. Essentially, they create their dance. To begin, ask your actor to flourish their arms and hands, experimenting with bold, sculpturing gestures and exploring the extensions of their body.

You are encouraging them to picture abstractly in movement their sense of the text phrase by phrase. It is wise to ask them to begin slowly. They need to first feel in their bodies and their voices the pulsations of poetic drama, the alternation of weak and strong accents, which are necessary to make the meaning clear. *Shakespeare Acrobatic* begins to unlock the information contained within the iambic pentameter form. The flow of the exercise then lunges the actor into psycho-physical actions.

Your actors can read about the technicalities of this process in many textbooks. They will carefully explain the basic Shakespearean line is iambic verse, which is a perfect analogy of the human heartbeat. In its pentameter line of ten beats, it begins with an unaccented followed by an accented beat. However, for many actors, in my experience, this is undigested information, until they discover it in the actions of their bodies.

This exercise should be done one on one with the actor and the director, removing their possible self-consciousness, rather than experimenting with it in front of the rest of the cast. I have had many actors have a major breakthrough, with this exercise, as a meaning of the passage of text is revealed through psychophysical principles.

Exercise #5
Paraphrase and Paraphrase Acrobatic

If an actor seems baffled over a substantial section of the text of Shakespeare or other verse plays, you might suggest the traditional research. You would urge your actors to use the dictionary and several different editions of the play to consult footnotes. You would further suggest that they write the troubling passage(s) of the text into contemporary language.

Hopefully, your actors will be able to respond in the moment if you ask them to paraphrase a section of the text in their own words. This exercise has another value as well. When the actor uses their own words, rather than the playwright's, quite subtly, they tend to invest a more personal stake in their character and the play's circumstances.

Another opportunity for the *Shakespeare Acrobatic* exercise is it may be used as a two-tiered experience for actors needing help. If there are cast members having problems with both the meaning and the rhythm of the text, you should do a paraphrasing "acrobatic" exploration of a passage, asking the actor to speak the text in their own words and move, as described in the Shakespeare Acrobatic exercise, to physicalize the piece. Having established a better connection of body and voice through colloquial speech, shift gears and ask the actor now to do the "acrobatic" using the playwright's words. They should now, having experienced both exercises, find a stronger personalization and a more poetic mastery of the text.

These techniques work equally well for an ensemble. You may want to spend some general rehearsal time introducing these ideas to your entire cast in-group scenes when you are rehearsing verse plays.

Finally, a cautionary word about paraphrasing. Some coaching directors use it extensively in all styles of theatre, including plays written in contemporary vernacular. The purpose, they suggest, is that the more the actors substitute their own words for the playwrights, the deeper they bond with the script. This idea has some validity. However, if paraphrasing is used for an extended amount of time in rehearsals, the actors tend to memorize their own, rather than the dramatist's words. It then becomes far more difficult for them, and the prompter, to do their jobs properly. The audience has come to hear the playwright's music. The actors and directors' goal should be a letter-perfect spoken text. I endorse paraphrasing, but not in excess.

9

Psycho Physical Ensemble

This chapter will deal with a multi-stepped technique that I developed a number of years ago and have used it with confidence in every production I have directed in all genres and styles of theatre production.

First, here is an exercise dealing with scenes of increasing emotional explosion containing intense hostility or violent outbursts in which actors may easily go over the top. This group interaction allows your actors to be powerful and build to a climax while maintaining emotional control.

Exercise #1
Anger Management

When audiences are asked to evaluate a play they have just seen, a frequent response, is, "I liked it except for the actors shouting at one another. It took me out of the play" Shouting is a recurring problem in productions because many actors lack a process to deal with a dramatic situation that grows in intensity and ends explosively. There is a procedure that directors have used to help their actors build a scene from a low-point to a climax. It involves the vocal elements of volume and pitch as well as tempo and intensity. A climactic scene is begun at a somewhat lower volume and pitch level than what has preceded it and then builds in a stair-step manner. Volume and pitch begin to rise as the tempo of the dialogue picks up speed. The actor's intensity then grows as more words are stressed in each phrase they speak. This progression builds to a crescendo at the climactic speech in the scene without actors shouting. This is the goal desired. There are, however, two potential problems here. This process may create actors body tension when ease and relaxation are most needed. Secondly, this vocal maneuver demands considerable concentration, which can result in the actors losing their inner connection to the world of the play's circumstances. It is a lapse that an audience may easily observe.

There is a simple organic solution to the problem that will prove far more effective. It is the use of a common household item - a bed, or a sofa pillow. In rehearsal, the pillow becomes the object of the character's anger as they slap or punch it on each line of dialogue. The actor's hostility with each other is absorbed by the pillow. This allows them to send their anger outward rather than their pulling it inside, increasing their inner tensions. Each hit of the pillow will build a character's growing anger toward the other characters in the scene.

Ask your actors to choose the greatest variety of physical actions on their attack of the pillow, ranging from soft to intense. The scene might begin with a moderate slap followed by a sharper more hurtful one. The blows will build in intensity, perhaps culminating in a quick succession of strong punches. Let the pillow absorb the hostilities as your actors assault it, either on the floor with them kneeling around it or elevated on a table with the actors standing.

Climatic scenes are generally short, usually eight to ten lines of dialogue, spoken by several characters. You will likely want to repeat this exercise several times for your actors to gain mastery of it. The first approach might be played as a game rather than concentrating on given circumstances. It could be a competition of the actors one-upping each other; each attack of the pillow will have an "anything you can do; I can do better" attitude. The final run would continue building passion but melding it into the circumstances and inner images of the scene.

The next run-through would be to remove the pillow and ask your actors to retain the sense memories they gained working with it as they play the scene realistically. At the conclusion they will have experienced Stanislavski's Psycho-Physical principle that "feeling follows action." You should find this exercise an ideal solution for the problem of actors building a scene to a climactic moment. It allows them to reach a smooth vocal peak without forcing or yelling.

We are approaching our key psychophysical exercise. It will be valuable as early as the first mini-unit is off-book, and prove vital until the end of the rehearsal period. The origin of this exercise has its own dramatic story and, as I tell it, you will understand its significance.

Some of the best moments in performance are the result of accidents in rehearsal. This one was a spellbinder. I was conducting the final run-through of Moliere's *The Learned Ladies* at a regional performance of the American College Theatre Festival. This event, as you may know, involves bringing a production from a home campus and performing it at another college or university on an unfamiliar stage with a single rehearsal for both a technical rehearsal and a final run-through of the show.

We had completed a cue to cue and were feeling reasonably confident about the tech elements. We now had two and a half hours allotted to us before a break and the evening performance. We had just launched our run-through when suddenly all the power in the windowless building failed.

The actors stopped the action of the play. It seemed impossible to continue in the dark. We patiently waited for the lights to be restored. After several minutes of darkness, with the clock relentlessly ticking away toward curtain time, I requested the stage manager flick his lighter. In that minimal light, I asked the cast to memorize the position of each of their acting partners, none of whom were more than a few steps away from one another.

I had a feeling, that if the actors knew their relative positions at this moment and would walk their blocking, but greatly reduced, we might be able to continue the run-through. I must have said something like, "keep a hand in front of you and move slowly toward the person to whom you are speaking and touch them for identification and mutual safety, until the lights come back on."

As the clock ticked on, the lighter sputtered out but the rehearsal continued. The actors walked their blocking, faltering at first with the restricted movement. In the darkness the actors identified their partners through touch as they spoke their dialogue. While the obstacle of the dark created a much slower tempo than the brisk comedy required, something remarkable was beginning to happen. As I stood downstage of my actors, I became aware of a clarity in communication and spontaneity I had not previously heard. I suspected it had to be their physical contact that brought about this perceptible change in their performance.

I halted the run-through again and, with more intuition than expertise, suggested that they keep their hands touching their partners throughout their entire speeches. Then, hesitantly, I suggested what I was later to realize was the key to this breakthrough. I told my actors to touch the hands, faces, shoulders, and torsos of their partners in a manner that might, in this sightless world they were in, *communicate what they were feeling at this moment about each other*. That is, were they friendly, hostile, warm, cold, angry, or at ease? Since their body language and facial reactions could not be seen, I wanted them to try to communicate with their sense of touch.

If what I had heard previously was greater clarity of the plot, the rehearsal now took on a further new dimension. There was a barrage of new impulses. The actor's relationships seemed strengthened and several *psychological actions* were changed; perhaps more remarkable, was the subtext of the scenes came through with a clarity it had lacked.

It was as if more progress was occurring in forty-minutes in the dark than in weeks in a lighted theatre. This experience was the catalyst that took solid rehearsal work and transformed it into something quite extraordinary. I stood near my actors in the dark with much admiration for what they were doing, but in all honesty, still with some confusion as to why it was occurring.

Then, with a great jolt, the lights came blazing on. There was a moment of silent awe. We blinked and then the actors in great excitement started talking all at once. They were eager to share their perceptions of this remarkable experience. "Yes," I said, "We must talk later." My first thought now was to pick up the continuity with full blocking where we stopped, then I suddenly changed my mind; I was too intrigued by this new creative event to return to traditional practices.

I knew this growth was not about the dark. It was about the touch. I asked the actors, in the time remaining to us, to break away from their set blocking and improvise their movements, continuing the sustained touch with one another. Now that we were in full light, the actors could look into each other's eyes. They could observe the facial expression and body language; but after their time in the dark, they had discovered the power of physical touch. As I watched the rehearsal continue with the security of light, the actors grew bolder. It was as if the sustained touch had become an instantly invented language. The actors with their fingers and hands applied to one another's faces and torsos, were expressing how they thought and felt about the other characters. When the actors would break the physical connection, which they were inclined to do when they concentrated on words only, they would lose the vitality and spontaneity their touch was creating.

I did a great deal of side coaching, urging the actors to keep touching on each line of dialogue they spoke. This tactile work was a new form of communication for them and, as with all new habits, it took some reinforcement and encouragement. As they progressed, the actors experimented with more full-bodied actions. For example, they hugged and embraced, or they would at first tentatively then more firmly push a partner away or pull one another closer to reinforce their character intentions.

We finished our run-through only minutes before our allotted time. What a whirlwind of a rehearsal it had been. There was now a dinner break, then the actors would be in the theatre for makeup, costumes, and performance. Before I dismissed the company, I knew I needed to speak to them about what I had observed at this remarkable rehearsal and help the actors process what they had done and how they might apply it in the performance ahead. I told them I thought they had discovered an intensive kind of sense memory that, through touch, was informing them of their character's feelings, relationships, and needs with a sense of immediacy and spontaneity they had not previously experienced. I thanked them for their commitment to the rehearsal, urging them to have a relaxing meal and then take some time to reflect on the process they had discovered together. They exited the rehearsal hall in high spirits.

I stayed behind, reflecting on the experience. I was in a more somber mood than my actors. Had I done the right thing when the lights returned to continue the touch rehearsal, as opposed to the more traditional wisdom of rehearsing the play as it had been staged? I was experiencing an all too familiar state of director nerves. What would be the outcome of the performance? I focused my thoughts back to the experimental afternoon rehearsal. What had I learned? Of what was I certain? I was absolutely convinced that the actors touching one another freely and sustaining the touch, led to the remarkable breakthrough in the rehearsal.

I recalled the theatre adage that your partner is your lifeline in the play. Yes, I thought, and you must cling to them for dear life. This may be a metaphor about acting, but I had experienced it as a reality in action. I felt calmer then and more optimistic. Before curtain time, I went backstage to wish the actors success; they were in an upbeat mood and at performance readiness. I exited to the back of the house to watch the show. Before the lights went to black, I decided whatever the results of the evening, I would continue to experiment with today's stunning discoveries.

Minutes into the performance, I realized I need have no doubts about the outcome. The festival audience was laughing heartily at Moliere's pretentious ladies from the outset of the play as the casts' skill and joy soared well beyond any previous performance. I was exhilarated by the day's events. At that moment, there could have been no way to know I would spend decades ahead using this technique in every production I would direct. As I continue to refine and use this process in acting classes and rehearsals, I look back with awe on the day I discovered a gold mine.

Exercise #2
The Lifeline (Warm-up)

Now that I have traced the background of this experience in some detail, we must explore a working approach toward its use in your rehearsals. Its application will be somewhat different from the other exercises in this book. First, it is the one ensemble exercise that will involve all your actors in a continuing process.

You should begin this key exercise in your initial rehearsals of mini-units and progress with it until the final run-throughs. Start with some preliminary warm-up aspects of *Lifeline* that will help prepare your actors for the boldness and freedom they will need as they engage in this initially unfamiliar tactile language. It should begin with some exercises you may have introduced in earlier rehearsals.

The warm-up will begin when lines are off-book for the first *mini-unit* of the text and the actors are secure in their lines. They should be seated on chairs or the floor in a closed circle. Actors exchanging dialogue together early in the scene should sit opposite one another. If there are cast members not in this *mini-unit*, they should observe the process behind the active circle. The entire cast must gain knowledge of this process from the beginning of the work.

The actors should be near enough to one another so that they can either move their chairs or propel themselves easily on the floor to their first speaking partner. The warm-up will proceed in several steps. The first speaking actors will sit with their knees comfortably touching their partner's. They should take about thirty seconds to establish and hold eye contact with them. To help achieve maximum concentration, I suggest they simultaneously scan each other's faces to discover a feature or quality they have not previously seen.

Then, keeping eye contact, ask them to imagine themselves as visual artists, planning to paint their partner's face. Now, each actor will reach out to their partner with open palms and fingers slightly spread. As they touch palm to palm, the first actor with dialogue begins to slowly speak their text while pushing their partner's palms back toward the other's chest. The partner reciprocates this move as they speak. Together they continue this process as if touch and speech were inseparable.

It is important here that your actors realize they are creating a new kind of language. They need to sense that there is an emotional connection between the words they utter and their mutual touch. The palm-to-palm touch needs to reflect the relationships and intentions at this moment of their characters' text or subtext, whichever is more important to the story.

Is the touch soft or harsh? Is the push smooth or staccato? Is it fast or lingering? The partner will return the touch as a response to what they have just received kinetically. If one character's response to a harsh is push is anger, the other might resist their partner, stiffen their hands, and refuse to return the push. The pair may need to stop, take a beat, and then begin again. Your cast will quickly grasp what is needed, in a given moment.

They are now ready to begin the next preliminary maneuver to gain an understanding of the process in *Lifeline*. Your actors will continue with the text, but rather than a palm to palm connection, you will ask them now to extend their touch to their partner's upper body. Remaining seated, each actor will touch their partner's face, arms, or torso on every line of their dialogue. The actors will need to continue speaking somewhat slowly to experience these sensations.

The challenge is to sustain touching throughout the entire line of spoken dialogue without stopping. The quality of the actor's touch must remain fluid throughout the line. A touch to the partner's body or face should explore the relationship and feelings that the speaking actor is experiencing at this specific moment. Among other options, for example as a character touches their partner's cheek, they may begin to pat, squeeze, massage, or caress for the duration of their spoken line.

I need to stress that you must not allow your actors to break the *Lifeline*. In this exercise, like its nautical namesake, if you let go of your *Lifeline*, you drown. Likewise, if the actor breaks their connection, they sink. Your actors need to train themselves to sustain their touch throughout all their spoken lines. They may be tentative in the beginning. You will likely be side coaching, "Keep touching," throughout the early stages of the exercise. They will soon discover there is extraordinary creative power in this sensory experience. However, if the touch stops, the power source is turned off.

Your actors' preparatory work is now accomplished, and the actors are ready to perform the full exercise. you need now to be in a space that has your ground plan to scale and all rehearsal furniture correctly placed. No props should be on the set–in order to ensure actor safety. In my earliest experiences with this process, there were a few minor scrapes as actors juggled set props with the *physical actions* involved in *Lifeline*. I then eliminated them, as they are unnecessary to the success of the work.

Exercise #3
Lifeline Run-Through

To begin your first full run-through of *Lifeline* off-book, ask your actors to sit in a circle in your ground plan space. Request that they begin the dialogue with sustained touch at a moderate tempo. The touching will again involve their partner's face and upper bodies. Then, let the actors ease into the scene by asking one character to find a motivation in the text to rise and assist their partner to their feet. Each continuing group will follow until all the actors are standing as the tactile actions flow forward and the actors motivate their established movement in the scene. Initially, the actors will be inclined to recreate their blocking. As they gain assurance, their touching responses will lead them to discoveries, different from the original blocking, which often will be more compelling and appropriate. Encourage your actors to take note of any changes so they can retain these moments, if you feel their newly discovered choices are stronger.

The actor's challenge now is how to sustain the touch whilst moving. A mundane choice like an arm on the shoulder of the partner as they walk to their next blocking position may be realistic, but it is not fulfilling the intent of *Lifeline*, which is to reveal character relationships and hidden subtexts in which psychophysical choices are sustained.

Continuing touch is the key to the process, more powerful choices will be discovered through pushing, pulling, dancing, boxing, or embracing their partners, as they move through their blocking. You should not need to give such specific directions to your actors. After a few trial runs, they will likely surprise you with their own original appropriate *physical actions*.

I have described this process in some detail, as I want you to understand how it works and picture how it will develop in future rehearsals. As you run these preliminary steps with your actors, you will discover that the warm-up steps can be achieved in less than ten minutes. Recall my story of the origin of *Lifeline*. In that highly pressured situation, my actors performed it as they invented it and that was in the dark! Your cast should have rapid growth and delight in discovering this most valuable tool.

After each brief *Lifeline mini-unit* run-through, you should share your observations while your actors catch their breath. The energy of a *Lifeline* run is intense. In specific moments where the cast made discoveries in their character choices, specifically point them out and ask them to incorporate that work in the run-through of the unit ahead. Your actors may wish to share their excitement about this invigorating exercise now. I recommend you postpone that exchange until after they repeat the run of the *mini-unit*. It is most important that they retain their creative discoveries and incorporate them in a traditional run-through at performance tempo with props before any new choices are forgotten. This run-through will give you and the actors welcome proof of the growth and progress, that they will achieve in LifeLine.

It has been my experience that after the first exploration of a *Lifeline mini-unit* and the traditional run-through that follows it, actors are eager to keep working with this exercise because of the creative stimulus it gives them. The *mini-unit*, ten to twelve minutes of text, is an ideal length to encourage this work. When your actors memorize the play in these short sections, a new unit is off-book every several days. In my rehearsal plan, I schedule *mini-units* so I can cover the entire play with *Lifeline* work in about four weeks.

A ten-minute *Lifeline* unit and a follow-up run-through of it, can be accommodated in any rehearsal. Your actor's skills in their touch vocabulary will grow with every new unit on which they work.

Stanislavski's units of objectives, which I refer to as *psychological* and *physical actions*, deal with left-brain intellectual activity, which is analytical, that *Lifeline* deals with intuitive spontaneous experiences, that are the function of the right brain. Actors use both sides in this process, as they complement each other.

The actors' physicalizing in *Lifeline* frequently deals with physical opposites to tell the story more clearly. Tactile maneuvers may involve:

Push-Pull

Attack–Retreat

Caress–Repel

As *Lifeline* rehearsals progress, you may wish to side coach, suggesting appropriate verbs when you sense your actors need to raise the stakes. They should work for bolder, more powerful Anglo-Saxon verbs, offer some suggestions. Literal physicalizing verbs like attack, push, strike, and kick are necessary to the visceral power of *Lifeline*, however the actors working so intimately together, must pull their punches to ensure a safe, protected acting environment. In decades of using *Lifeline*, I have not experienced a single actor injury.

Here are some verbs to introduce to your actors, that are powerful and vivid without being overly intense:

Press

Flick

Slither

Float

Tap

Dab

Rub

Sculpt

Now I want to offer two further aspects of psycho-physical exercises that your actors may incorporate in this work. These techniques may be explored separately and then combined in the original *Lifeline* exercise.

Exercise #4
On with the Dance

As the actors study a script, they may encounter an extended section that has the quality of a dance. Using *Lifeline*, they can experience the play's rhythms physically in either traditional or improvised steps. Their imaginations will ignite when you ask them to move together responding to the musicality in the play's story. It is the discovery of the rhythms, not the accuracy of execution that is important.

"Hold tight," cries a familiar lyric from the swing era. The physical connection of *Lifeline* permits the actors to engage in turns, twists, circles, and other maneuvers while clinging fast to their partners. A particular section of the text may suggest the hyper-quality of the jitterbug, the slow sensuous rhythms of a waltz, or the dynamic beat of hip hop. In a waltz, the actors might be moving cheek to cheek as one partner, softly whispers their dialogue into the partner's ear. Dance movement can reveal both moods and relationships in a scene that might not otherwise get fully explored.

A major advantage of dance in the traditional *Lifeline* exercise is that it becomes a basic mode of transportation as one actor leads, whirls, or pushes the partner to the next location in the blocking without breaking their physical connection.

Exercise #5
Lifeline Zoo

Another alternative to *Lifeline* is animal characterizations. There is a long history of actors basing their characters on an animal. Perhaps the first recorded was the 19th-century Italian actor Salvini, who chose to play the character, Othello, as a tiger. In the early 20th century, the Russian actress Nazimova offered her Hedda Gabler as a panther. The tradition continues in contemporary acting.

When an actor is committed to a full-scale animal characterization, considerable observation and research is necessary. Extensive viewing of the animal in action, wildlife films, and visits to zoos are part of the preparation. For our purposes, as a supplement to *Lifeline* work, it will, by necessity, be a shorter procedure based primarily on your actors' imaginations. The values for them in this work will include increased power, an interesting eccentricity in character choices, different body centers, and heightened sensory awareness.

The actors should choose an animal that intrigues them and should have some specific qualities and associations with their character. Give them time to prepare as they close their eyes and open their imaginations. Ask them to concentrate on some elements: the lines of the animal's body, the energy it takes in moving its limbs, the rhythms of its movements, how it distributes its weight, the sounds it makes, its manner of attack, and its behavior in retreat.

To begin the exercise, the actors will go to the ground and crawl on all fours to explore their animal bodies in action. Give them time to make physical discoveries. As they move in their habitat, they should experiment with sounds in varying moods from aggression to contentment, that the animal would make. At this point, they should be alone in their world. Interaction will occur in the *Lifeline* exercise. You might ask them to experience a *phys-*

ical action with each of their five senses. What do they touch, taste, see, hear, and smell? What sense is strongest? Which is the weakest?

As the actor slowly rises on two legs, they will regain their own human body and characteristics. They should work in their imaginations to recapture approximately 80 percent of their human character, preserving 20 percent of their animal behavior.

As you begin the *Lifeline Zoo* exercise, there will be a degree of suspense, as the partners do not know what animals they will be facing. It can be an exciting work-through of discoveries. Warn your actors, however, to avoid overly intense aggressive behavior. Any hostile moves should be carefully controlled.

Quirky, original choices will occur as the sense of touch takes on a new dimension. Remember, in this *Lifeline Zoo*, the characters are essentially human, so the basic form of the exercise will remain the same. The 20 percent animal behavior can however reveal unexpected creative results. Some of these choices will likely remain as exciting performance moments in your finished production.

Lifeline has ranged over a considerable period of time for me, from a long-ago rehearsal in the dark, through many years of my actor's experiments and refinements. You will be using the exercise as you move first through run-throughs of *mini-units* and then proceed to longer sections of the script. You should consider both *On with The Dance and Lifeline* Zoo, as changes of pace and a means of discovering different aspects of character behavior.

In the next chapter, I will discuss rehearsal schedules, goals in run-throughs, and maximizing rehearsal efficiency.

10

Putting It Together The Rehearsal Process

We enter now the final phase of our rehearsal process. In this two-and-aa- half-week period, you will alternate between concentrated coaching in polishing rehearsals and a series of complete run-throughs, leading into tech and dress rehearsals.

A predominant emphasis of this chapter will deal with helping you develop a comprehensive rehearsal plan. In the opening chapter, I spoke about some commonly accepted requisites of a director's work. The first was Leadership and Organization, no aspect of the organization is more crucial than the formulation of a detailed rehearsal schedule. You will need to create a comprehensive strategy that builds actor morale, sustains their interest, offers a logical progression in which the actors can realize their growth, and uses their time efficiently.

While this preparation is fundamentally important, it is often taken for granted. I would hope to remedy that by offering some specific strategies that will guide you in creating your own detailed rehearsal plan.

Have you ever seen a play with a promising first act? The show seemed well enough staged, energetically paced with competent acting performances, then after intermission it all fell apart? In the second act, some of the blocking appeared unmotivated, acting choices were tentative and the actor's voices were indistinct as they seemed to be fighting just to remember lines. It was as if you were seeing two different productions of the same play; one had been well prepared, the other was sloppy and amateurish.

An untrained audience leaving the theatre might be greatly confused about what they had just seen. Can you define the problem? Yes, the director had spent the majority of rehearsal time on the first act, perhaps with repeated run-throughs for the actors to gain confidence. Then, in the waning days of the allotted time, work was begun on the last act, but it was too late. The production opened and it was a train wreck. While this might seem like an elementary time management error a thoughtful director would not allow, in actuality it occurs too frequently. It is the downfall of a director who has not pre-planned their work and begins directing their actors without a schedule containing specific goals for every rehearsal. It may be tempting to embrace the attitude of, "Let's see where my actors get to today, then I will think about tomorrow's rehearsal." As coaching directors, we are accommodating and sensitive to our actor's needs, but it is a disservice to fail to inform them of the next day's work so they may prepare specifically for it. Directors should have the overall plan of rehearsals in their actor's hands at the outset of the work.

Think of it as the architectural plan of the play you are building. Like the structure of your text, the rehearsal schedule has its own rhythms. It starts slowly as you lay the foundation, guiding your actors in exploratory exercises. It gains momentum as they investigate improvisations and have a change of pace as the actors analyze their psychological and physical actions and blocking choices. It slows a bit as the actors struggle to learn their lines, then gains speed as they run mini-units and later, longer sections and acts. Then polishing rehearsals challenge them to probe deeper and helps them discover their choices and images that will enrich their roles.

Your actors will have multiple advantages with a schedule in their hands at the first rehearsal. As they read through it and understand their total time commitment to the production, they make a tacit agreement to fulfill it. With a specific schedule, they can prepare as you have, but for their characters. It further provides the opportunity to clear in advance any conflicts they might have with it. Adjustments in the schedule are possible, especially if they are made at the outset of rehearsals. You will have indicated all the "lines off" deadlines, including those for mini-units. These shorter sections make it far easier for your actors as they work to get off book and it keeps the morale high. Yes, there will be more deadlines than in the traditional model where directors often wait for the actors to memorize a full act before scheduling an off-book run-through. More deadlines, of short mini-units, will ensure greater efficiency and faster progress. Most important, it is far less stressful for your actors. When a lengthy section or a full act is called off-book, actors are likely to stumble under the burden, repeatedly call for lines, and at the end of the rehearsal feel frustrated about both their work and the show's lack of progress. The actor-director coach is always alert to building positive morale in rehearsals and should work to avoid such possible negative perceptions.

It is advisable as well to give a copy of the rehearsal schedule to each member of the design team. This alerts them to the dates of partial or complete run-throughs they may wish to observe. In consultation with them, you should agree on design element deadlines. Some should be possible before dress rehearsals, thus removing some stress from this always intense event. For instance, it is important to have mockup prop deadlines for the mini-units. They should be scheduled for the second or third running of the material after the actors are off-book. At this point, they are, relatively secure in their lines and will profit working with mockup props. Handling them earlier allows them more time to develop creative character choices with them.

Technical rehearsals will progress more efficiently if other design elements have some preliminary deadlines. The sound designer's job will flow more smoothly if they work in the house for several rehearsals with the actors on the timing of the sound and music cues. Costumes will be kept on target by your presence at actors' fittings and a cast costume parade as the actors try on all their clothes so you and your designer may preview them from the house, approximately ten days before the first dress. Lights will progress much faster at the first technical if one or more "paper techs", moving verbally through all the cues with the stage manager, director and lighting designer, in a session are conducted.

By scheduling the mini-unit runs, complete run-throughs are unnecessary until your actors are completely off-book. This normally happens in the fourth week of a six-and-a half-week schedule. These run-throughs will alternate with final polishing rehearsals. I recommend eight to ten nonstop run-throughs, which will include two or three dress rehearsals.

Normally, equity union actors rehearse for 4 weeks but work 6 to 8 hours daily, racking up from 144 to 192 hours of rehearsal time. It is logical then that your actors should come close to that amount of time spread over six and a half to eight weeks to develop their roles. I suggest a model of forty to forty-five rehearsals, working three and a half hours daily, six days a week on a full-length play. This formula will need to be adjusted depending on the complexity of additional production elements such as song, dance, combat, and length of the script. I want to suggest now another efficient approach for a smooth progression of your rehearsals. Like the mini-unit it is a process of dividing the script into smaller portions. Why make another division? The play is already divided into acts and possibly scenes as well. That is the actual problem. When directors attempt to complete long passages of text like a lengthy scene or an act in one rehearsal, there is not sufficient time to explore it in depth. If directors rush through it, the actors can't process it properly. I want to suggest that you work instead with two kinds of divisions: a longer one that we will call a *section* and the shorter *mini-unit*, with which you are now familiar. These two-elements will complement each other. The five-step-mini-unit is the most efficient and in-depth approach to your rehearsal process as it combines script analysis and blocking simultaneously. Ultimately, it will save you valuable time. Initially, because of the larger quantity of mini-units, your blocking time will be longer than in the traditional method, but you have the advantage of a deeper exploration of the play. Your actors will have leaped ahead of those working in the traditional process.

You will, likewise need a method of reviewing earlier mini-units as you move forward creating new ones. In my experience, actors need to review earlier blocked material every three days. It is counterproductive if previous units are not regularly revisited. It will result in actors losing some of the verbal and motor skills they have acquired; consequently, their work will take a backward step. This wastes time and can sabotage actor morale.

A section will be comprised of three *mini-units*, perfect for the three-day review process. A *section* will consist of approximately fifteen pages of the script. With an estimate of a page of dialogue running two to two and a half minutes, a section run-through will take approximately 35 to 45 minutes to play. This leaves you about 20 minutes to give notes and make minor adjustments. A one-hour *section* run-through is a wise investment of time for every rehearsal, in which you explore a new mini-unit, that will run approximately two hours. This combination of rehearsing a new *mini-unit* and a section is, particularly productive as you move the play forward, while reviewing earlier text in the same rehearsal.

To determine the running time of a *section*, break the script into divisions of thirteen to seventeen pages so the sections will average fifteen pages. Partitioning the script in this manner is strictly a numerical exercise. Your actors will have no trouble with continuity; just be sure to finish a complete action *beat* at the cut-off page. Determine the total number of *sections* by the number of pages in the script. A brief ten-to-fifteen-minute one-act play would need 1 *section*. A conventional one-act of 30 pages would equal 2 sections. A short full-length play of 45 pages would require 3 *sections* and the sixty-page play, 4 *sections*. A maximum of up to 6 *sections* can work well. For scripts of greater lengths, more sections are needed. The director will need to consider adding more time to the rehearsal schedule to make the process workable.

These section rehearsals work well to increase your actor's energy and build stamina in the rehearsal process. As you have increasingly fewer new mini-units to cover, the ratio of the mini-units and the *sections* will reverse. Your rehearsal might then include two-section run-throughs and one new mini-unit. The rehearsal of the mini-unit will have become more compact at this point as you have concluded with the improvs, unless needed and the other elements are in all probability moving faster as your actors have more mastery of this process.

These section run-throughs, will build your actors continuity, confidence, and the pacing of the production. When the first complete run-through occurs, your actors will have infinitely more authority and expertise than actors in traditional rehearsals, who will likely consider their first off-book complete run-through a daunting experience. You may want to look again at the five-step process of the mini-units in Chapter 5 before you begin this work with your actors. Here is a summary of the process.

1. *Discuss It* (20 minutes)

Your actors read the five-page scene. You ask questions about the when and where. Determine the major *given circumstances* of the unit.

2. *Improv It* (15 minutes)

Choose one situation from the past life of major characters. The actors improv the incident to begin to learn the backstory, subtext, and character relationships. Discuss actor discoveries.

3. *Action It* (30 minutes)

Determine the character's needs in the scene. Explore verbs that lead to the *psychological actions* of the characters. Work to achieve the strongest verbs. Experiment with the *physical actions* that demonstrate the character's needs.

4. *Stage It* (30 minutes)

Collaborative actor and director blocking occur when the director encourages the actors to follow the impulses their verbs suggest. They should experiment with different choices. The director is prepared to offer blocking directions if the actors falter, and will suggest some stage business and actions, for them.

5.   *Run It, Evaluate It* (25 minutes)

Work for nonstop run-throughs. Make blocking changes if needed. Be positive about what is working. Give feedback on what to prepare for in the next rehearsal of the unit.

Now let me pause a moment to explain my seeming emphasis on the ticking clock. You may be thinking at this point that your author has some kind of compulsive time disorder and is urging you to have your stage manager note each minute of the rehearsal with a stopwatch and push a buzzer if a unit runs overtime. I assure you that is not my intent. Careful, time management in each rehearsal will play a significant outcome in the quality of your production. A reliable timetable must be working in your head. You need to be able to estimate the time allotments for each of the five steps of the mini-units as you proceed with your work. Avoid frequent glances at your watch, or worse yet, announcing to your cast in a pathetic tone, "we are behind schedule." Such behavior will only give your actors anxiety. Trust yourself that you can work within these general time guidelines. Be assured that if a portion of the rehearsal runs overtime, another will be under. If you are in harmony with your inner clock, creative rehearsals will flow naturally. The "mini-unit" and "section" are new concepts as they have not been publicized. I urge you to experiment with them both because I am confident that the resulting more rapid actor growth, efficiency, and time saved in rehearsals will greatly benefit your directing process.

Let us consider now some other aspects of the coaching director's leadership as we look at our ethical responsibilities to our actors and how we build company morale. The British director, John Fernald, spoke with wisdom when he said, "What gives actors confidence and ensures they will give their best to a director is not the amount of fluency of his direction but the faith he can inspire that what he says is true." The coaching director needs to assume many different roles for their actors: cheerleader, critic, best friend, psychologist, but above all, we must strive to be honest. That does not mean offering unrelenting criticism. It means building the skill of knowing when to offer actors positive comments and when critical feedback is essential. There is some truth in the directing adage, praise in public, criticize in private. Certainly, if an actor is having serious problems with their role, the director should speak to them privately and offer coaching solutions. However, excessive praise in public is not always the best strategy.

I once observed a production where the director praised his actors fulsomely and assured them that they were building a truly beautiful production together. In the early stages, there was a good spirit; the cast trusted him. As time passed, and the show didn't grow, morale began to decline. The director, although personally in near desperation, continued to assure his cast that it would be wonderful. Of course, it wasn't. Resentment toward the director was widespread among the company. On the other hand, directors with sharp tongues must learn to curb them. As a coaching director, you should understand that you hold a position of considerable power with your actors, and with that power comes a significant responsibility. To engage in a company, note session with an actor in sarcasm, to ridicule their mannerisms or interpretations, is the behavior of a bully, not a coaching director. Neither unwarranted praise nor hurtful criticism will build morale in rehearsals. Rather the coaching director needs to create an attitude of patience tempered with gentle persistence and honesty to succeed in his work.

Another rehearsal essential for you as a coaching director is a high energy level. Again, director John Fernald explains, "Physical vitality is one of the director's most precious assets. Without this, his knowledge and his understanding may fail to make themselves felt. A tired director lets small indulgences go by without summoning the energy to interrupt. A bad production is often no more than a succession of small inadequacies." The director's energy is contagious to his actors. He sets the standards and the pace of the work. George Cukor, the highly esteemed Hollywood film director, offered a pithy metaphor, when he said, "When the director sits down, the actors sit down."

George Bernard Shaw, the famed playwright, often directed and then published his advice to directors. In his signature comic tone, he told us, "Don't mention trifles such as; slips in business, or words, in a heartbroken desperate way, as if the world was crumbling into ruins. Don't mention anything that doesn't matter." Strive at note sessions to offer at least one response to every actor in a scene. This may be difficult with your best and most experienced actors. But it is most important that you do. There is frequently a complaint by skilled actors, that directors spend the bulk of their note sessions on directions to the less experienced cast members, consequently ignoring them. This can become a moral problem.

If you have no critical feedback in a session for your most skilled actors, be sure to verbalize positive input for what they are doing. Don't let them become victims of benign neglect. The coaching director needs to build a positive spirit in note sessions from the first one to the last dress rehearsal. That is achieved by giving your actors a balance of honest constructive criticism along with praise, when it is earned.

While I have waited until this point in the book to discuss the presentation of company notes, this process for the coaching director begins very early in our rehearsals. It should most likely begin with the first run-through of a mini-unit off-book. Your ability to take and present notes to your cast will be an important skill you develop throughout your rehearsal process. I would recommend that you give your actors a ten-minute break after any full run-through. During this time, you should review and revise your notes. If in the run-through an actor is having a difficulty, which would be best solved in a coaching exercise rather than a prolonged conversation. Put a star by the note indicating you will speak to them after the rehearsal to set a time to work together on the problem.

When you take a note for every trouble spot you see and hear, this can make for long note sessions after a run-through when actors are tired. You may wish to work with some alternative procedures. Consider limiting your notes to forty-five minutes. If you have not finished at that time, you may release your cast and send your notes via email or another electronic method. This works well up to dress rehearsals. The actors should have a full day to process their notes. Therefore, complete oral note sessions are recommended at each dress rehearsal. Hopefully, by this time the critical notes are few and your overall attitude exudes a sense of positiveness and calmness as the leader of the pack. When you might be distressed in a rehearsal, follow Hamlet's advice to his mother, "Assume a virtue, if you have it not." The virtue is to always keep your cool.

In your brief time revising your notes, you may find that you cannot read one or more of them. Cross out any unintelligible notes. Don't waste time and your actor's patience by stumbling over a note and then apologetically announcing you're sorry you can't read it. If those lost notes are serious issues, they will resurface again, and you will have another opportunity to solve the problem.

You should continue to evaluate how your cast can better tell the play's story. Before each final run-through, you should choose a particular goal or problem for your actors to work on and solve. This offers them incentives to grow the production. It can bring energy to run-throughs that your actors may be taking for granted or, worse yet, scenes that have gone stale. Here are some strategies to keep the actors' concentration and morale building.

Exercise #1
The Play in a Foreign Language

Gibberish, the actors speaking in their own invented language of nonsense syllables, can create a new stimulus with their partners, as the cast must work to communicate the play to each other in an improvised language. If actors have become too comfortable and seem to be on autopilot, speaking gibberish will require greater attention to their partners. They must reconnect and rely on making their *psychological actions* clear so they know what they need from each other despite their speaking in a "foreign language". This exercise can be a challenge, but actors have the advantage of knowing their story well, and if they rely on each other, they will create fresh energy and hopefully new choices. Because of the intense concentration required, this exercise might best be used in the mini-unit format, then return to the traditional run-through process.

Exercise #2

Tightening the Text

It is four nights before you open the play. You have just finished a complete run-through. You are pleased with the moment-to-moment work of your actors. You have, however, a sinking feeling that the show is far from ready to open. Each recent run-through has been growing longer than the previous one. You are suddenly aware the production is dragging. It has a deadening slowness. What now?

First, you must identify the problem. It is not that your actors aren't picking up their cues; that is a problem that happens with beginners, and if that were the difficulty you would have seen it and fixed it earlier. It is much subtler than that. Be prepared for a shock. You, as a coaching director, maybe part of the problem. You have been working with your actors on beats and pauses at the end of them. They have been working on filling them with their images and subtext. This is essential in our way of working. It may, however, have become seductive for the actors in their enjoyment of this process.

Consequently, there is an over-indulgence of images and the pauses have become extended beyond the length of an audience's acceptance of a dramatic moment. You appreciate your actor's internal work, but now you are jolted to discover that the production has become lethargic. If you panic and tell your actors to speed up, much of their careful and precise work will be lost. Don't lose hope; there is a simple solution. Explain to your actors they are going to have a *tightening of the text* run-through. Be clear in explaining that they are to cut nothing. All their creative work is to be retained. However, the pauses between the beats will have a sharper mental pace and therefore be shorter. The actors will quicken their sensory perceptions and subtext to gain the audiences complete attention. This adjustment will greatly energize the production, the actor's faster mental agility will enliven moments that have become ponderous. As you challenge your actors to quicken their responses to stimuli, you may be surprised at their acceptance and realization that dropping the extra weight from their lengthy pauses will heighten their performance.

To be certain your actors understand that what you are asking for is not speeding up and blurring of beats, but rather a more agile mental process that burns off excess fat, you should ask them to run a few trial beats to be sure your entire cast is on the same page and understands the process involved in *Tightening the Text*. After this run-through, minutes will have been dropped from the production and the actors will delight in their sense of achievement as they realize the show's progress.

Exercise # 3
Returning To LifeLine

This exercise, which will have delivered such productive results throughout your rehearsal process, will again demonstrate its reliability, re-invigorating your actors in the crucial final days before opening. It is powerful in its basic format, but you should consider working with *On With The Dance* and *LifeLine* Zoo, as well, particularly if you haven't had an opportunity to use them earlier. *LifeLine* is the gift that keeps on giving. No repetition of it is ever identical. Each rendering brings subtle changes in character relationships and offers the actors greater physical freedom. Again, as in, The Play in a *Foreign Language*, a full run-through can exhaust the cast. One mini-unit should provide the spark needed to re-invigorate the remainder of a traditional run-through.

Exercise #4

Revitalizing the Concept

Throughout the rehearsal process you have been working with the actors to make the story of your play clear and compelling to your audience. Now, as opening night approaches, it is wise to review with the cast your major thematic ideas for the production.

In your early exploratory rehearsals, you had a concept session, ideally with your designer's present, in which you offered an interpretation of the play. It may be your view of the playwright's intention when they wrote it, or it may be your choosing contemporary social or cultural themes that you feel gives the play relevancy now. This process, you remember, often called the CONTROLLING IDEA or COMMANDING IMAGE is offered in metaphor or a concise conceptual statement. The actors have lived with this image or concept throughout rehearsals. How has it influenced the work on their characters?

I suggest just prior to opening that you discuss with your cast reviewing and hopefully revitalizing your concept for the actors. They must get in touch with the feelings they experienced when first introduced to the concept and recognize how their understanding of the play and personal journey with it has influenced the performance they are about to present.

Exercise # 5

Envision Victory

Your official directing duties are completed. However, your cast will expect to see you on opening night before the play begins. Certainly, you will want to thank them for their talent, time, dedication, and hard work. To illustrate better what you might share with them, let us take a quick imaginary trip from the green room to the baseball dugout.

The home team is trailing with a score of three to nothing in the bottom half of the ninth inning. The manager gathers his first four batters and asks the first three to picture getting a base hit. They must go through a movie in their minds, experiencing the balls and strikes that get them each on base. They succeed. The manager then whispers to the fourth player that he needs to visualize hitting a home run. He goes to the plate, lobs the ball out of the park, and with the bases loaded, the home team wins the game 4 to 3. A pleasant fantasy? Actually, this is a technique developed by sports psychologists to win games. The description, dealing with imagination and moment-to-moment images, sounds like an acting exercise, which of course, it is. I suggest we reclaim it as actor coaches for our team of actors to energize their opening. Ask your cast to form a circle, join hands and close their eyes. Tell them to imagine the final scene of tonight's production; they should experience the deep satisfaction resulting from a near-flawless performance, their best ever. Take a moment to get in touch with that thought and find the power in it. Sense the electricity in the audience, caught up in rapt involvement as the lights go to black. Ask your actors to experience this and then sustain for a lingering moment their personal feelings of accomplishment and joy in the performance. You may wish to create your version of this improv, that can deliver a calming sense of accomplishment to balance your cast's opening night energy levels.

In your journey within this book, you have traveled from the first spontaneous impulse reading of the play to the exploratory rehearsals that led to textual breakthroughs using improvs. Recall your discovery of a new five-step mini-unit approach to staging that allowed actors to analyze their characters while they simultaneously block the play. Polishing rehearsals offered a multitude of exercises and theatre games to solve actor challenges in concentration, connection, and vulnerability, among other challenges.

Psycho/physical work then offered actors full freedom of their bodies and *Lifeline* gave them the boldness and power to make their performances exceptional.

It is time now for you to find your play, your cast, your space, and enter into the unique satisfaction of becoming a coaching director.

List Of Exercises, Improvs And Games

3
IMPROVISATION

4
EXPLORATORY REHEARSALS

6
IMAGINATIONS AND IMAGES

7
PLAYING IT TOGETHER

7
PLAYING IT TOGETHER

(Continued)

8
PSYCHO PHYSICAL SOLO COACHING

9
Psychophysical Actor Coach Ensemble Work

10
PUTTING IT TOGETHER
REHEARSAL PROCESS

Bibliography

Adler, Stella, The technique of Acting,
Bantam Books 1988

Ball, William, A Sense of Direction
Drama Book Publishers, 1984

Benedetti, Robert L, The Director at Work,
Prentice Hall, Inc. 1985

Benedetti, Jean, An Actor's Work
A contemporary translation of An Actor Prepares and
Building a Character, Routledge, 2008

Boleslavsky, Richard, Acting The First Six Lessons,
Theatre Arts Books, 1949

Bentley, Eric, Bernard Shaw, A Reconsideration,
The Norton Library, 1975

Checkhov, Michael, To the Actor,
Harper & Row, 1953

Caldarone, Marina & Maggie Lloyd Williams,
Actions the Actor's Thesaurus,
Nick Hern Books, 2004

Clurman, Harold, On Directing
Collier Books, 1974

Cohen, Robert- John Harrop, Creative Play Directing,
Prentice Hall Inc, 1974

Cole toby-Chinoy Helen Krich, Directors on Directing
Bobbs-Merrill 1963

Delgado, Ramon Acting with Both Sides of Your Brains
Holt, Rhinehart and Winston 1986

Fernald, John, Sense of Direction, the Director & his Actors
Stein and Day, 1969

Hagen, Uta A Challenge for the Actor
Scribner's Charles and Sons 1991

Hull, S. Loraine, Strasberg Method
Ox Bow Publishing Inc, 1985

Johnstone, Keith Impro,
Theatre Arts Books, 1979

Jory, Jon Tips Ideas for Directors
Smith and Kraus, 2002

Kazan, Elia Kazan on Directing,
Vintage Books 2009

Lewis, Robert, Method or Madness,
Samuel French Inc, 1958
Leiter, Samuel L, The Great Stage Directors
Facts on File, 1994

Meisner, Sanford, Meisner on Acting
Vintage Books, 1987

Moss, Larry, The Intent to Live,
Bantam Books, 2005

Pasolli, Robert, A Book on the Open Theatre,
Bobbs- Merrill Inc. 1970

Roberston, Warren, Free to Act,
G.P. Putnam's Sons, 1978

Rosenstein, Sophie, Modern Acting; A Manual
Samuel French, 1936

Rossi, Alfred, Astonish Us in The Morning
Tyrone Guthrie Remembered, Wayne State University Press, 1980

Rotte, Joanna, Acting with Adler
Limelight Editions, 2006

Silverberg, Larry, The Sanford Meisner Approach Workbook Two, Smith
and Kraus Inc, 1997

Smith, Wendy, Real Life The Group Theatre and America 1931-1940 Alfred
A. Knopf, 1990

Tairov, Alexander, Notes of A Director
University of Miami Press, 1969

Weston, Judith, Directing Actors, Michael Wiese Productions, 1996

About The Author

Forrest Sears received an MFA in directing from the Yale School of Drama and began a five-decade career, directing some 130 productions. He co-founded the Sears-Whiteside Acting Studio and Repertory Theatre in San Francisco. Later, he joined the company of the Pittsburg Playhouse as an actor, director, and acting teacher in their professional training program.

Professor Sears then enjoyed an award-winning career at the University of Idaho, where he chaired the acting and directing programs. He received multiple awards from the American College Theatre Festival. Five of his productions were selected and performed at ACTF Regional Festivals. Four of his students were national Irene Ryan recipients, honored in their performances at the Kennedy Center.

Sears was presented with the Mayor Award in Arts education and the University of Idaho's Teacher of the year award. Forrest was recently presented with the Gold Medallion Award by the Kennedy Center for his lifetime of service and contribution to the Theatre.

He has taught abroad for the Canterbury Drama League in Timaru, New Zealand, and presented a course in American Method Acting at the professional Actor Training School in Tampere, Finland.

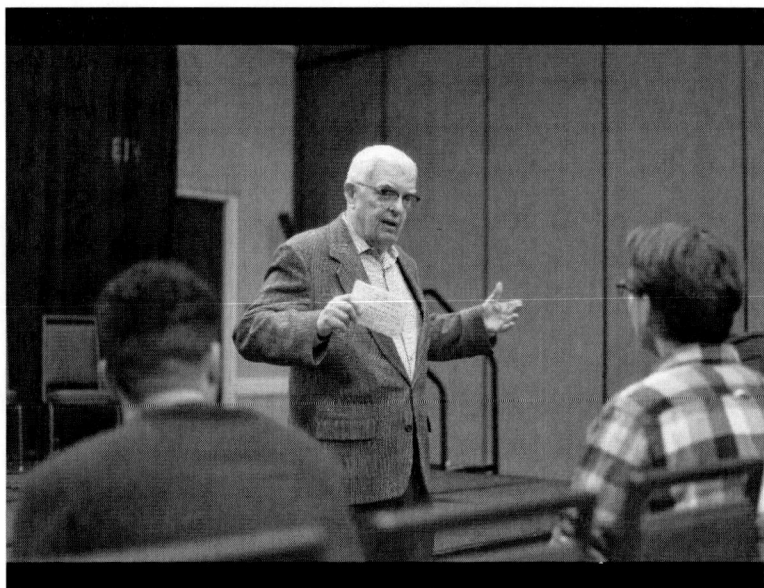